On the Trail of Big Cats

Acknowledgments

I want to warmly thank Remy Marion and Francis Petter without whom I would not have been able to write this book.
G.V.

Work prepared with the assistance of
Anne Cauquetoux
Stephanie Houlvigue

Iconographic research
Remy MARION

Illustration sources
(as listed)

Title of original edition: *Cap sur les Félins*
Published by Les Editions Nathan, Paris
French edition by Géraldine Véron, Illustrations by Robert Dallet

All inquiries should be addressed to:
Barron's Educational Series, Inc.
250 Wireless Boulevard
Hauppauge, NY 11788
http://www.barronseduc.com

Library of Congress Catalog Card No. 98-4548

International Standard Book No. 0-7641-0597-3

Library of Congress Cataloging-in-Publication Data

Véron, Géraldine.
[Cap sur les félins. English]
On the trail : big cats / Géraldine Véron ; illustrations by Robert Dallet.
p. cm. — (On the trail series)
Includes bibliographical references (p.) and index.
Summary: Discusses the physical characteristics, behavior, habitats, and ranges of lions, panthers, jaguars, and other large wild cats.
ISBN 0-7641-0597-3
1. Felidae—Juvenile literature. 2. Wildlife viewing sites—Juvenile literature. [1. Felidae. 2. Cats.] I. Dallet, Robert, i11. II. Title. III. Series.
QL737.C23V4713 1998
599.75'5—dc21.
98-4548
CIP
AC

Printed in Italy
9 8 7 6 5 4 3 2 1

Géraldine Véron

Illustrations by Robert Dallet

Contents

Bardia
Gir Forest
Kanha
and Bandhavgarh
okolo Koba
Masai Mara
Ujung Kulon
Hwange
Etosha

Foreword

Symbols of nobility and strength, cats occupy a special place in the minds of humans. Found the world over, these animals, frightening but above all fascinating, have a place in our mythologies. They entered human history as predators. Very quickly, however, the roles reversed and cats became the object of mass persecution. The habitats in which they live are now increasingly destroyed and their prey, victims of hunting, are becoming so rare that today many species of cats are highly endangered.

To see such predators places us in direct contact with the laws of nature, with its violence and, from an anthropomorphic point of view, cruelty. This book invites you to discover the fascination cats hold for us so they might be loved, protected, better understood, and simply admired for their beauty.

The first part of this book overviews the cat family's characteristics from a physical as well as a behavioral perspective. The next part describes all of the species of big cats. Six among them—the cheetah, lion, leopard, tiger, jaguar, and puma (also called the cougar)—are treated in more detail. A description of each cat's lifestyle and physical characteristics is included, as well as suggested observation sites, travel information, and practical information to give you the best chance of meeting these great wild cats.

Originally, the first cats were forest animals; they then spread to many other habitats. Some, like the tiger, live in habitats that are not very accessible to humans.

INTRODUCTION TO CATS

Origin and evolution

All present-day carnivorous mammals, or carnivores (order *Carnivora*), have a common ancestor related to the miacids that appeared approximately 60 million years ago. A branch among them evolved toward the *caniforms*, a group characterized by an undivided or only partially divided tympanic bullae at the level of the middle ear (*canids*: dogs and foxes, and *arctoids*: bears, weasels, pandas, and raccoons). Another group of miacids gave rise to the *aeluroids* or *feliforms*, that have a true septum (partition having a double origin) in the tympanic bullae; felines, as well as hyenas, mongooses, civets, and genets belong to this group.

Carnivores have kept certain characteristics inherited from their common ancestor which are theirs alone. For example, the fourth upper premolar and the first lower premolar were transformed into *carnassials*, powerful cutting teeth with reduced grinding capability. The diverse adaptations that evolved within the families of carnivores have sometimes modified the original design. That is true of seals, whose diet of fish or krill has brought about a complete dental change. On the other hand, felines that specialized in preying on large animals developed stereotypically exaggerated carnivorous characteristics. In other words, they developed large stabbing teeth.

Felines (the *Felidae* family) appeared approximately 40 million years ago, with an animal called *Proailurus*. Later, *Pseudaelurus* developed. The fossils of these animals show characteristics typical of the feline family, such as extreme development of the cutting portion of the carnassial teeth, a total reduction of their grinding portion, and the reduction of the molars. The *Felidae* include modern-day species but also certain saber-toothed cats such as *Smilodon*, whose last members became extinct approximately

Small cats are represented throughout the world (except Australia). A large number of them are Asiatic (Asian golden cat, fishing cat, reddish cat . . .), some of them are African (African golden cat, black-footed cat, Margueritte's cat), and others are South American (ocelot, pampas cat, Andes cat, kodkod, Geoffrey's cat and margay—photo above). Wild cats had a wide distribution in the Old World.

10,000 years ago. These felines survived by evolving an efficient means of killing prey. This unique technique is due to their adaptive musculature and honed senses. The canines were long enough to slip between the cervical vertebrae of the prey and assure a rapid death. This bite to the neck is efficient and precise.

Molecular evidence has allowed researchers to estimate the dates at which the different lines diverged, and this has provided us a theory on feline evolution. The first separation took place about 12 million years ago and gave rise to the small cats of South America (the ocelot, margay, little spotted cat, and Geoffrey's cat). The second line separated 8 to 10 million years ago, and from this line came the small wild cats (the jungle cat, sand cat, black-footed cat, and Pallas's cat). Four to six million years ago, a third line diverged and provided the golden cats and the puma. Finally, only 3.8 to 1.8 million years ago, the lion, tiger, leopard, jaguar, and lynx developed.

Classification and division

The *Felidae* are broadly divided into the pantherines or large cats, and the small cats. All 37 species (more or less depending on the author) are spread throughout the globe. In America, the majority of felines inhabit Mexico, and Central and South America (the jaguar, jaguarundi, ocelot, oncilla or little spotted cat, and margay), with certain cats confined south of Latin America (the pampas cat, Andes cat, Geoffrey's cat, and Kodkod). Numerous species can be found in Africa (the lion, leopard, jackal, serval, African golden cat, wildcat, black-footed cat, and sand cat). Asiatic species often have narrow ranges (the Asian lion, tiger, marbled cat, clouded leopard, snow leopard, Asian golden cat, Bengal cat, fishing cat, flat-headed cat, rusty-spotted cat, Borneo golden cat, Iriomote cat, Pallas's cat, and jungle cat); some species are Eurasian (Eurasian lynx, European wild cat). The widest range is that of the leopard *(Panthera pardus)*, which is found in Africa as well as in a large portion of Asia.

The evolutionary development of *Felidae* according to Herrington, 1986

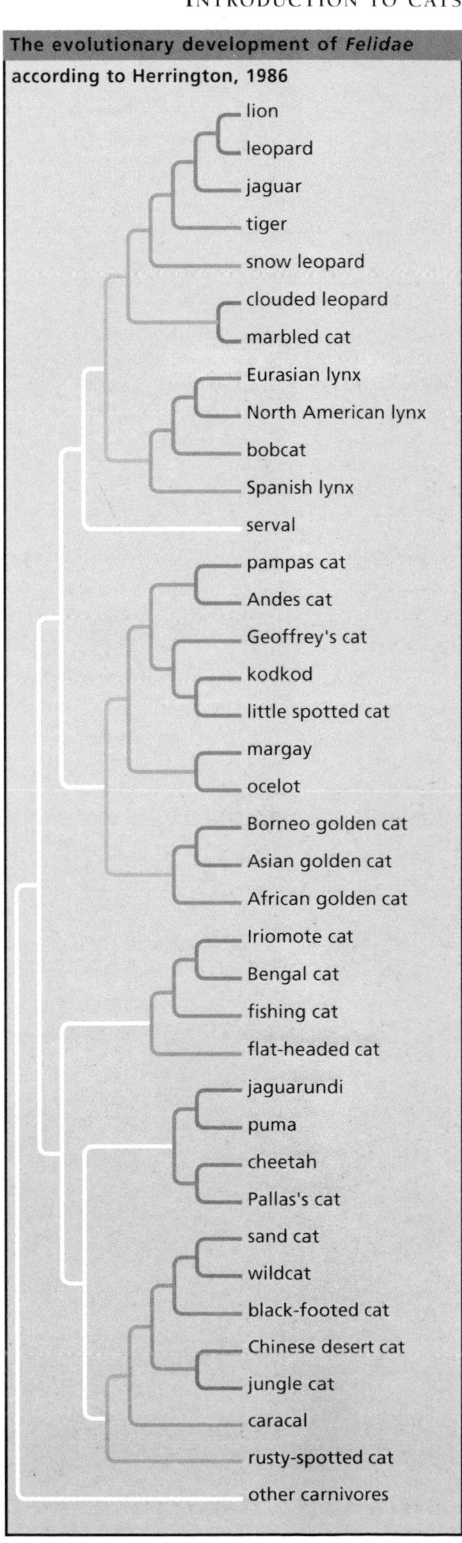

Cats have inhabited practically all environments, but the majority of them live in forests. Many species are active and hunt at night, or at dawn and twilight; some hunt during the day, like the leopard. Their hunting patterns generally follow that of their prey, but it depends also on environmental and climatic factors.

Physical description

The cat's **length** (the body including the head) varies from (2.80 m) (tiger, *Panthera tigris*) to 14 in (35 cm) (rusty-spotted cat, *Prionailurus rubiginosus*). Usually, the ears are small and rounded, sometimes topped by a tuft of fur (lynx, caracal). The body is long and supple and the long tail gives the body additional length, except for the lynx, bobcat, and their relatives, whose tails are bobbed. The marbled cat has the longest tail proportionally; the tail of this small feline of Southeast Asia measures from 14–22 in. (35–55 cm), whereas the length of its body (including the head) is between 16 and 24 in. (45–61 cm)

The **fur color** of the cat's back and sides is generally tawny and the underbelly usually whitish. In many species, the coat is spotted or striped. The supposed role that these coats play in camouflaging cats has not been completely explained; the stripes present an advantage in grassy habitats or underbrush because they resemble the vertical patterns formed by vegetation; the spots provide good camouflage for felines living in trees because they imitate the shadows of the leaves. Nevertheless, solid-colored species also seem perfectly suited to their environment and are able to hide themselves just as well. The young of certain solid-colored species, such as the lion and the puma, have spotted coats. On the other hand, the young of cheetahs are born practically solid in color. Researchers have developed theories concerning the evolution of feline fur markings; they surmise that the initial coat type possessed dark spots which could either have joined to become stripes, or paled in the center to form the characteristic rosettes of leopards and jaguars, or disappeared entirely to be replaced by a solid coat. The numerous color and pattern varieties chosen by domestic cat breeders show the feline potential for variety; the fur color for different species was determined by natural selection according to habitat, hunting habits, and social behavior.

The lynx and the caracal have a neck ruff; male lions possess a full mane that develops with age. This mane is a secondary sexual characteristic; apparently its role is to make the individual appear more impressive than he really is. It is also an immediate indication of age, social rank, and state of health. During confrontations between males, the mane also prevents claws and teeth from easily reaching the sensitive parts of the head.

The rhinarium (the hairless area at the tip of the muzzle where the nostrils open) does not extend beneath the nostrils, and this is unusual. The moustache and whiskers are well developed, although under-the-chin whiskers are absent in felidae.

Melanism appears among many feline species, a frequent mutation in humid habitats (here, a black leopard).

Sexual dimorphism generally is not very significant among felines, except among lions whose social status is established by rank and individuality. This dimorphism (where the male and female are dissimilar in appearance) is common among felines, usually in size and weight. In the puma species, for example, males weigh 147–227 lb (67–103 kg) whereas females weigh 79–132 lb (36–60 kg).

Coat color polymorphism exists among felines. The species with the most variable color is probably the African golden cat, whose color varies from orange to gray and whose coat can be solid or partially (or even completely) spotted. Variations in coat and color in species like the wildcat are related to geographic region, with solid, lighter colors in the drier regions, and darker, spotted, and striped forms in humid zones. Further, wildcats that live in Africa and Asia have shorter fur than those native to Europe. Another variation found quite commonly in felines is melanism (dark or black pigmentation in the skin and fur), the most well known and frequent being the black leopards common in tropical forests. The phenomenon occurs also among jaguars, kodkods, Geoffrey's cat, and among solid-coat species like the caracal, the golden cats, and the jungle cat. Melanism seems more frequent in tropical and forest habitats than in dry, open habitats.

Felines have short, large muzzles. Their eyes are directed forward, permitting better binocular **vision**, which is important for a predator. Their carnassial **teeth** (fourth upper premolar and first lower molar) are well developed and cut like the blades of a pair of scissors. The jugal teeth (molars and premolars) other than the carnassials are smaller or have disappeared, leaving thirty (twenty-eight for the lynx and Pallas's cat), compared with the canine's forty-two teeth, for example. The articulation of the jaw permits only vertical movements, since lateral movements are useless to carnivores. The canine teeth are long and pointed. This cranial and dental development is linked to their adaptation for preying on large animals. The canines permit the cat to kill its prey, and the carnassials help the cat tear the prey's flesh. The jaw's great muscular power heightens the carnassials' efficiency. Due to the disappearance of the teeth normally found behind them, the carnassials are situated very near the hinge of the lower jaw, providing greater scissoring force.

The felines' short muzzle makes them more efficient predators than, for example, the canids. A roughly similar development is found among hyenas (hyenides), whose jaw strength and carnassial development allow them to grind large bones. The **digestive system** is simplified, as it is among all carnivores but particularly so among felines,

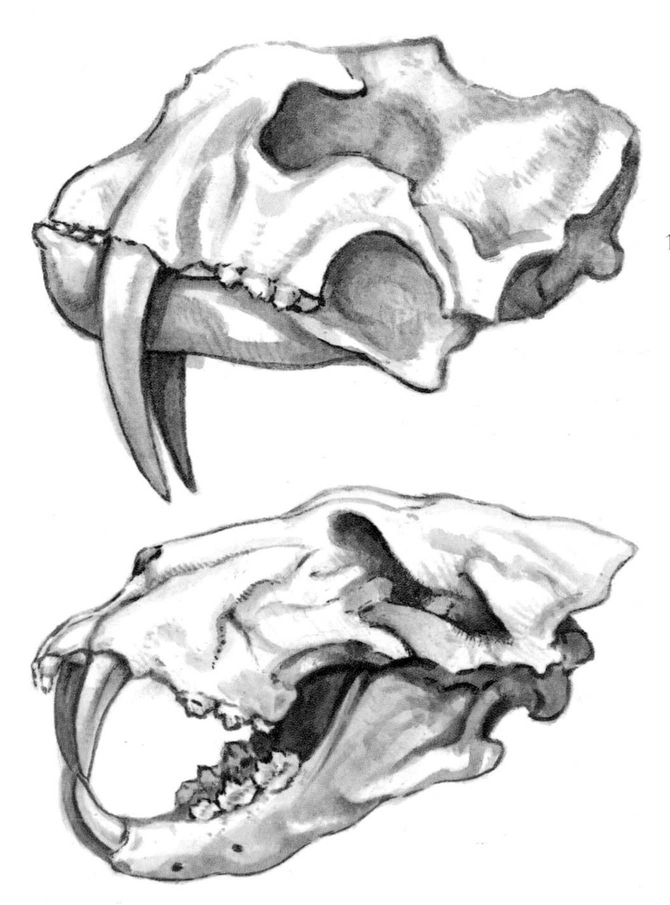

Felines have adapted to prey on animals of great size (bottom, a lion skull). The development of the canine teeth was extreme in some fossil groups (top, a *Smilodon*).

given their exclusively carnivorous diet. The tongue is covered with backward-pointing spines that help rasp flesh off the bones of their prey.

Movement

Cats are digitrade, which means the body weight rests on the toes rather than the heel of the foot. The fifth claw on the front foot (the cat's "thumb") does not touch the ground and the first toe of the hind paws has disappeared. To facilitate running, the cat has developed longer, slimmer legs. The flexibility of the backbone and the freedom of movement of the omoplate (due to their smaller collarbone) also contribute to the cat's speed. Except for the cheetah and to a certain extent the fishing cat, felines possess fully retractable claws, perhaps developed from their tree-dwelling lifestyle. These claws allow them to catch and hold prey.

The fastest land mammal is the cheetah whose structure and physiology are extremely well adapted to the speed necessary for its hunting style. It approaches its prey slowly, then rapidly sprints after its intended victim; these chases generally don't last more than a minute. This extreme specialization has disadvantages: the energy expended by the cheetah's lightning sprint—that can reach 72 mph (120 km), is such that the animal must wait a good while before it is able to hunt again. Due to this rapid fatigue, approximately half of the cheetah's chases fail to bring down the intended prey.

Certain cat species are good swimmers. The tiger and the jaguar, for example, can swim long distances and often live near moving bodies of water. The leopard, in contrast, although completely capable of crossing streams, does not go out of its way to swim. The leopard inhabits a variety of habitats from dense forests to open plains, and can live in both humid and dry conditions. It climbs well and often drags its prey into trees in order to avoid scavengers. The jaguar is also a good climber. The puma, however, is essentially adapted to jumping rather than climbing: its rear legs are long, which allows it to be as comfortable in a forested habitat as on mountainous or irregular terrain. The small species are frequently good climbers and usually live in forests.

Senses

The cat's eyes are large, and the ability to see in near-darkness is heightened by the presence of a *tapetum lucidum*, a layer of cells behind the retina that reflects light and bounces it back to the light-sensitive cells in the retina. This gives felines good nocturnal vision. Small cats have vertical pupils, which are able to constrict more completely than round pupils.

Felines have efficient hearing and can hear higher frequencies of sound than humans can perceive (up to 70 Hz for the domestic cat). However, their hearing is less efficient in low frequencies. Although much more acute than ours, the feline sense of smell appears

Almost all cats are solitary. Generally, we know little about the social life of small cats like this jungle cat.

to be less efficient than for, say, canids, but data in this area is scarce.

Lifestyle

Social organization and behavior

Almost all felines lead solitary lives; the social organization for many species of small cats is not well known. The most complex social structure known is found among lions, which form groups of three to 30 individuals organized around related lionesses.

Territorial marking is done with urine, feces and, as among other carnivores, the secretions of the anal glands. Urine spraying is often accompanied by raking the ground with the claws. Large cats do not bury their feces; small cats do, and only within their territory.

Felines are equipped with glands at the base of the tail, the anus, the forehead, the side of the mouth, and the chin; they spread their scent by rubbing against stationary objects and other members of their species. Overall, however, olfactory communication is not as consequential in cats as in other animals.

Vocal communication, however, is well developed in cats. It is often combined with other forms, such as visual and olfactory communication. In general, sounds are produced by vibrations of the vocal cords during exhalation. The sound frequency is usually between 50 and 10,000 Hz. The loudest sound produced by any of the cat species is the roar of a male lion, registering 114 decibels. Certain sounds are made by all felines, while others are exclusive to each species. The calling meows are common to all species, although their intensity varies according to circumstances, even within the same species. Sounds made when a cat confronts another animal are almost always accompanied by visual signals, such as body posturing or facial expressions. In these situations, all cat species spit, hiss, or growl. In friendly situations, the sounds emitted are short, low-pitched, and loud. These sounds include gurgling (the majority of

The kill is perfected among cats. It is done by a bite of great precision at the nape of the neck or by a bite to the throat which chokes the prey.

cat species), snorting (clouded leopard, snow leopard, tiger, jaguar), or panting (lion and leopard). Purring is another sound emitted in friendly situations; this sound is produced during exhalation and inhalation and can last several minutes. It is frequently used by both mother and kitten or cub, and serves to reassure both. While purring, the cat can produce other sounds.

The lion, leopard, tiger, jaguar, and snow leopard are the only cats that can roar, due to the thickness of their vocal cords and the structure of their hyoid bone, which has more cartilage than in other species. It has been said that cats that roar do not purr and vice versa, but researchers are currently revising their opinions on the subject.

Cats use **scratching** as a means of communication. It leaves visual marks on objects for other cats to see, and also imparts the cat's scent because of the scent glands on the bottom of the feet. **Mimicking** and **posturing** are other visual signals often used in association with vocal communication. To show aggression, felines growl, erect their ears, turn sideways, constrict their pupils, and lash their tails furiously. To show submission, felines flatten their ears and dilate their pupils. Felines have specific, well-defined body postures to indicate both attack and submission; among animals capable of killing prey much larger than themselves, they prefer to clearly show their aggressive intentions rather than take the risk of a combat that could result in injury or death.

Sometimes, when a feline sniffs a scent marking or the genital-anal area of a member of its species, it remains in a particular posture, with lips curled, mouth open, and eyes fixed. (This is called the flehmen response.) This brings the odors into contact with the Jacobson's or vomeronasal organ situated between the nose and the palate, which is connected to the roof of the mouth by a duct located behind the upper incisor teeth. The organ gathers tiny chemical molecules from the odors it transmits directly to the brain. Researchers do not clearly understand this organ's purpose, but it is thought to be sexual in nature.

The female may couple with several males before being fertilized.

A large part of the feline's day is spent **sleeping** (up to eighteen hours). A carnivorous diet has the advantage of being rich and easy and quick to digest, which allows carnivores to eat infrequently, whereas herbivores must feed almost constantly. Furthermore, since predators of large cats are rare, constant vigilance is not as necessary as it would be for certain hoofed animals, for example. Also, the immense effort of the hunt must be compensated for by long periods of rest.

In lion prides, the females are usually the **hunters.** As a group, they circle their intended prey, which increases their chances of a successful hunt. When killed, the prey is devoured by the entire pride. Lions also feed on carcasses, unlike the cheetah who hunts alone, in sight of its prey, and consumes only animals that it has just killed. Tigers stalk their prey, and their strength allows them to attack large animals. The prey is most often seized with the paws; the claws play an important role in restraining the animal. The tiger delivers the fatal bite to the nape of the neck. Some felines search for specific prey, which they locate, stalk, and pursue; others wander about and throw themselves on anything that turns up. Certain species are more opportunistic than others and less selective in the choice of prey. They are thus less affected by the scarcity of any particular species of game.

Reproduction

In solitary species, the reproductive period is one of the rare moments of contact between members. The male approaches the female and smells her pheromones to determine her state of sexual receptivity. In small-cat species, the male grasps the scruff of the female's neck with his teeth and maintains his hold throughout the coupling. In large species, the male grasps the female for a short time only, then releases her for the remainder of copulation, perhaps to avoid injuring her. During copulation in the solitary species, the horned spines present on the penis stimulate the female's vagina, triggering ovulation. After coupling, the male and female avoid one another. The length of gestation is related to the size of the animal and can be from 66 days for the smallest cats to 103 days for the largest, which in this instance is the tiger. The female bears from one to four young, who are blind at birth. Commonly, she raises her young alone. Each kitten or cub selects a nipple for its exclusive use to avoid conflicts. Depending on the species, the eyes generally open when the cub is several days to 2 weeks of age.

The young are **socialized** and trained to hunt through play. When the young are several months old, the female brings them live prey so they can learn the necessary capture-and-kill techniques. Later, they accompany their mother on the hunt to perfect their skills. They leave her when they are one or two years of age, depending on the species; in general, they do not become adults until later. At first, the young form groups and wander together before establishing a territory or, in the case of lions, becoming part of a pride. Thanks to these associations, the young can become proficient hunters, reach a certain maturity, and acquire good physical strength before passing truly into adulthood.

Young felines are victim to numerous predators and illnesses, so that few of them survive beyond 3 months of age.

LARGE CATS AND HUMANS

In the past, a balance between animals and humans existed in **Africa**. The animals began to decline after the arrival of the Europeans because of intensive hunting and destruction of natural habitats. In addition, at the beginning of this century, wild animals were considered carriers of diseases that killed hundreds of thousands of domestic animals, and cats suffered the consequences of this belief. During the 1930s, a growing awareness brought about the creation of wild animal preserves and the restriction of trade in wild animal products.

The human population explosion in Africa is having a disastrous effect on the natural environment; destructive practices include slash-and-burn agriculture, overgrazing and the resultant soil erosion, using brush fires as a herding technique, poaching, animal trading, pollution, and urban development. Protection for animal species is often very inadequate. In certain cases, traditions and traditional religions make up for the lack of regulation. Other beliefs, however, do great harm, such as those touting the so-called aphrodisiac properties of certain animal organs.

Today, preserves from which humans were originally excluded are generally open to the public and have become places where plant and animal protection and the local human populations have found a balance. In fact, if protecting animals and their environment is financed with the help of wealthy countries, protection takes priority above all other considerations thanks to education. The creation of preserves has permitted tourism to develop, but this contributes to protection only if it is financially profitable to the local population. Tourism in certain parks of Africa is harmful to the animals. The number of vehicles in certain areas is so great that cheetahs, for example, are forced to hunt in full midday when the tourists are resting, which fatigues them enormously. Some visitors pursue the animals or try to photograph them close up, which is harmful to the animals' tranquillity. It is better for visitors to be equipped with a pair of binoculars or powerful telephoto lenses; moreover, observation is more interesting when the animals are disturbed as little as possible.

In North America, European colonization, with its intensive fur trade and economic development, reduced the wild animal populations to the point that at the end of the last century many species were on the brink of extinction. The beginning of the twentieth century brought an awareness of the urgent need to protect wild animal populations, and this led to the creation of natural parks. Certain species of cats had, however, already disappeared from numerous regions, particularly in the East.

Almost all cat species are endangered—victims of the fur trade, the disappearance of their prey, and the dwindling of their natural environment.

In Europe, conservation efforts started more recently and human pressure is stronger, which leaves little place for wild animals, particularly the great predators. Euroasiatic felines, the Eurasian lynx and the wildcat were still very widespread in the Middle Ages. The wildcat became rare because of the disappearance of its forest habitat and systematic trapping. In France, the wildcat has been protected since 1979, and is therefore no longer threatened with extinction. The lynx was also the object of such persecution that during the seventeenth century in France it was found only in the high mountain ridges and, over the following centuries, only in the Pyrenees. Beginning in the 1950s, its numbers have stopped dropping; the lynx reappeared in the Jura in 1974 and in the Alps in 1975 thanks to reintroductions which took place in Switzerland. It was also reintroduced in the Vosges mountains beginning in 1983, although not without difficulty.

In Asia, poor economic conditions and human overpopulation make problems of animal conservation particularly difficult. Despite this, protection projects have been implemented. In India, for example, a program called the Tiger Project was established to protect the tiger, made difficult by the danger that this large predator represents. The Asian lion has been protected since 1913; at that time only twenty or so still existed since they had been all but wiped out by hunting. Protection measures arrived a bit late and despite an increase in the number of individuals, it will be difficult to save the species. The snow leopard, which inhabits the mountains of central Asia (Siberia, Mongolia, China, Nepal, Bhutan, India, Pakistan, Afghanistan), is also one of the most endangered cats. Very localized, it lives above the forest line and is very difficult to study since it is so rare and shy. Until several years ago, nothing was known about its biology, which fueled local beliefs that the snow leopard sucked the blood of its victims. This species is classified as disappearing by the International Union for Nature Conservation (IUNC), and certain biologists feel that only 5,000 individuals are left. It is not only hunted for its fur and killed by cattle raisers, but is also victim to the scarcity of its prey. The scattered distribution also prevents contact between individuals from different populations, hence endangering the species' survival.

These examples demonstrate the problem of cohabitation between cats and humans. It is difficult to reconcile economic development and industrialization with the presence of large predators who need natural environments and game. In the poorest countries, the competition between cats and humans is even more evident and, in these cases, the losers are both the humans and the animals.

After the prohibition of trade in furs of the great spotted cats in 1975, the number of small cats killed, such as the lynx, rose. Thousands of skins are still sold every year.

RARE OR DIFFICULT-TO-OBSERVE LARGE CATS

Only the large cat species not discussed elsewhere in this book are described here.

The Clouded Leopard

(Neofelis nebulosa)

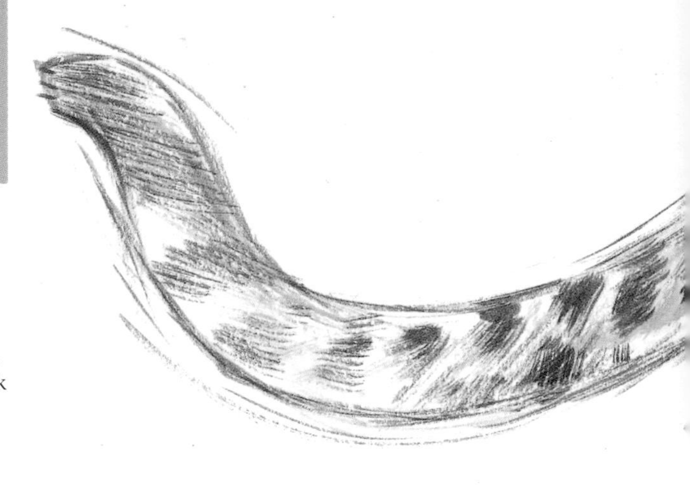

Description. This leopard has a powerful body, short legs, and a long tail. The flanks are decorated with large spots with dark edges and a lighter central portion. Its legs are covered with dark spots and the back is adorned with longitudinal bands. The undercoat is brown, gray, or yellow, and the underside is lighter and spotted.

Length. Head and body length 24–44 in (60–110 cm); tail 24–36 in (60–90 cm).

Weight. 33–48 lb (15–22 kg).

Lifespan. Up to 17 years in captivity.

Diet. The clouded leopard chiefly eats various birds, monkeys, squirrels, deer, wild boar, and porcupines.

Reproduction. The gestation period lasts from 85 to 90 days. The female most often bears two young (in general, from one to four) in the spring. Nursing lasts approximately twenty weeks. The young are active at 5 weeks and independent around nine months.

Lifestyle. A good climber, the clouded leopard (or longibanded leopard) can descend a tree head first. It is active at twilight. In its natural environment, the clouded leopard's social behavior is practically unknown as it is very shy and has rarely been observed in the wild.

Population. The species is considered vulnerable by protection groups, due to destruction of its habitat (deforestation) and to hunting for its fur.

Distribution. It is found in southern China, Bangladesh, Bhutan, Brunei, Cambodia, India, Indonesia (Kalimantan, Sumatra), Laos, Malaysia, Burma, Nepal, Taiwan (population possibly extinct), Thailand, and Vietnam.

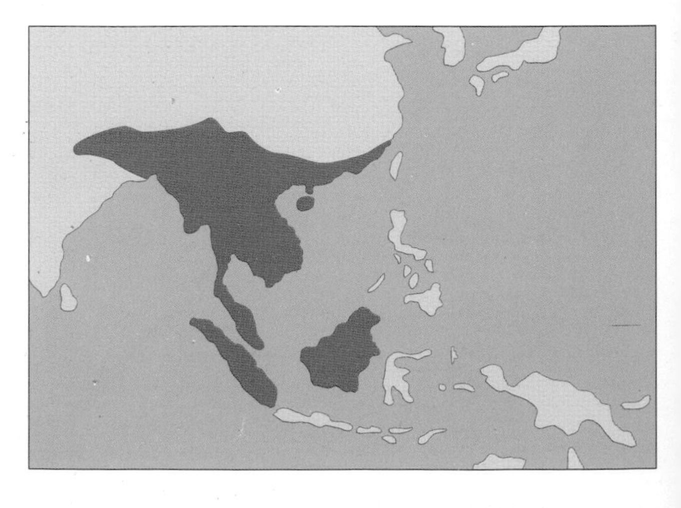

We know little about the lifestyle of the clouded leopard. Its claws are retractable, like those of other felines except the cheetah, and are used for climbing as well as for holding prey.

The Snow Leopard

(Uncia uncia)

Description. Also called the ounce, the snow leopard has a long, low body with strong legs of medium size; its small, round head is topped by short rounded ears. Its tail is long and well furred. The long, thick coat is light gray sprinkled with large black rosettes on the back and sides and a good portion of the tail. Black spots adorn the legs; the stomach is white. The winter coat is lighter in color.

Length. Head and body length from 40–60 in (100–150 cm); tail 32–40 in (80–100 cm).

Weight. 55–165 lb (25–75 kg); newborn 13–24 oz (368–708 g).

Lifespan. 15 years in captivity.

Diet. The snow leopard's diet mainly consists of woodchucks, bharals or blue sheep (*pseudois mayaur*), Asian ibex, hares, mice, and birds, but it also preys on domestic animals. In the winter, the snow leopard primarily eats wild boars, deer, gazelles, and hares. It supplements its diet with willow branches.

Reproduction. Gestation lasts from 98 to 103 days. Between April and June, from one to four young are born; they generally open their eyes when 8 days old. At approximately 30 days, they begin to eat solid foods and are weaned at around 8 to 10 weeks. They follow their mother to the hunt at 3 months and leave her when approximately 2 years old.

Lifestyle. The snow leopard is solitary and active at dawn or twilight. Its territory extends over roughly 12 sq mi (20 km).

Population. This species is endangered and estimates of the number of remaining snow leopards vary from 4,500 to 7,500, probably including only 2,500 adults. The nature of their habitat makes their distribution very scattered. They are threatened by the fur trade and by excessive hunting of their prey.

Distribution. Generally, the snow leopard lives at altitudes of 8,910–19,800 ft (2,700–6,000 m). It is found in Afghanistan, Bhutan, China, Kazakhstan, Kirghizia, Mongolia, Nepal, Pakistan, Russia, Tadzhikistan, and Uzbekistan.

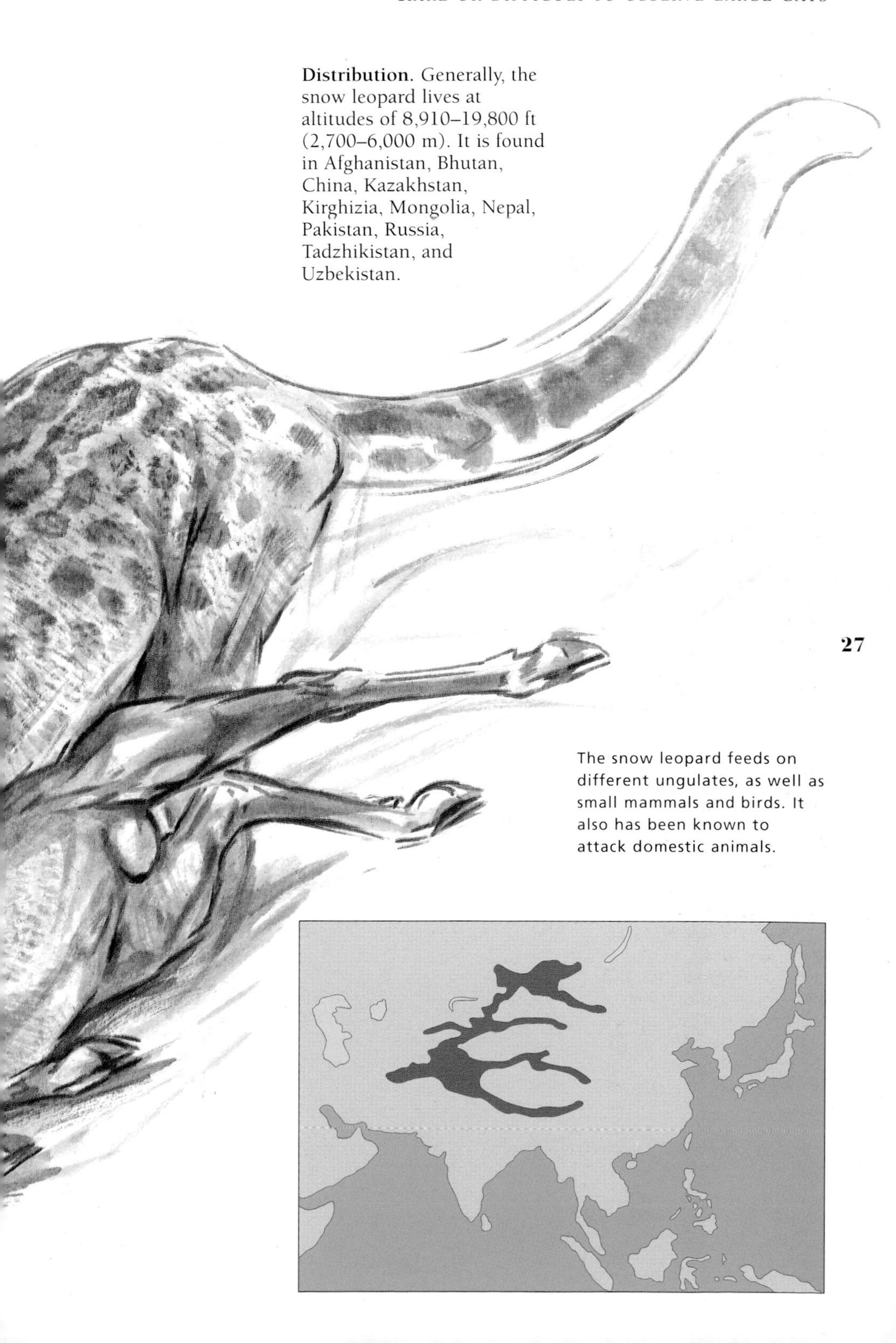

The snow leopard feeds on different ungulates, as well as small mammals and birds. It also has been known to attack domestic animals.

The North American Lynx

(Lynx canadensis)

Description. The North American lynx's rear legs are noticeably longer than those in front. Its neck bears a full ruff, and its ears are topped by black fur tufts. Its paws are wide and well furred, rather like snowshoes, to help the lynx walk on snow. Its tail is very short. Its long, thick fur is yellow-brown and spotted.

Length. Head to body length 32–40 in (80–100 cm); tail 2–5 in (5–13 cm).

Weight. Males are approximately 22 lb (10 kg); females are around 18 lb (8.5 kg); newborns are about 7 oz (200 g).

Lifespan. Up to 24 years in captivity. In the wild they live five to seven years, but exceptions are possible: a lynx of seventeen years has been captured.

Diet. The North American lynx primarily eats hares, but also will eat mice, voles, red squirrels, flying squirrels, and grouse, as well as deer and caribou (both fawns and adults). It does not generally eat large prey and only rarely attacks animals larger than itself, such as the white-tailed deer.

Reproduction. Gestation lasts 9 weeks; litters are generally born at the end of May or the beginning of June. The litter usually includes from two to four young; their eyes open 12 to 17 days after birth. They are weaned at approximately 3 months, and are capable of reproducing at one year, but usually wait until they are 2 years old to begin mating.

Lifestyle. The North American lynx is a solitary forest animal. It is active at twilight and at night. Its territory generally extends over 12 sq mi (20 sq km) and at times much more, especially for males.

Population. The North American lynx is not a threatened species. Nevertheless, the destruction of its habitat due to urban development causes loss of available prey, which creates disappearances on a local scale. Trapping is authorized outside the protected reserve and park areas.

Distribution. Alaska, Canada, and northern United States.

Lynx are recognizable by the tufts of fur on their ears, by the collar around their necks, and by their short tails.

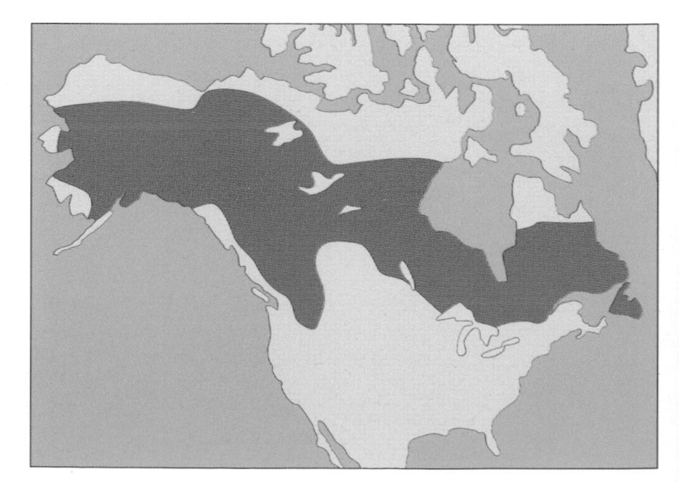

The Eurasian Lynx

(Lynx lynx)

Description. The Eurasian lynx is larger than the North American lynx but similar in appearance. Its fur is marked with black spots.

Length. Head and body length (80–130 cm); tail (11–24 cm).

Weight. Male about 44 lb (20 kg) (occasionally up to 84 lb, 38 kg); female about 37 lb (17 kg); newborn 7–11 oz, (200–300 g).

Lifespan. Up to 18 years.

Diet. The Eurasian lynx feeds primarily on hares and rabbits, but also on mice, birds, and at times on deer and cattle.

Reproduction. Gestation lasts 60 to 75 days; the female gives birth in May or June to a litter of one to four young that will open their eyes 10 to 12 days after birth. They begin to eat solid foods at 4 to 6 weeks, and are weaned at 5 months. They reach sexual maturity between one and a half and two and a half years of age.

Lifestyle. Lynx are good swimmers and climbers; they live primarily in forests with dense underbrush. They are solitary and can occupy a territory of several square miles; they are shy and are generally active at twilight and during the night.

Population. The Eurasian lynx is not considered an endangered species, but its numbers have decreased and it has disappeared completely from numerous areas in western Europe. It is hunted for its fur and also because it is blamed for killing game and domestic animals.

Distribution. The lynx was reintroduced into France, Germany, the former Yugoslavia, Switzerland, Italy, and Austria; it is also found in Scandinavia, Russia, Asia Minor, Iran, Iraq, Asia to Manchuria, Mongolia, and in the mountainous regions of central Asia.

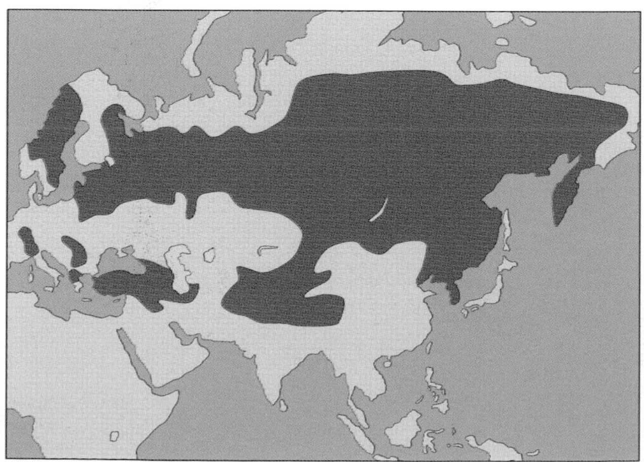

The Eurasian lynx resembles the American lynx, but is a bit larger.

The Spanish Lynx

(Lynx pardinus)

Description. This lynx closely resembles the North American lynx and the Eurasian lynx, but its coat is more vividly and densely spotted. Some researchers consider the Spanish lynx part of the species *Lynx lynx*.

Length. Male head and body length 39 in (98 cm); female head and body length 33–35 in (84–88 cm).

Weight. 26–29 lb (12–13 kg) for males and slightly less for females.

Lifespan. Unknown.

Diet. The Spanish lynx primarily feeds on wild rabbits, but also on ducks and deer fawns.

Reproduction. Similar to that of the Eurasian lynx.

Lifestyle. The solitary Spanish lynx usually lives in wooded mountain areas. It is difficult to observe because it is very shy, and is nocturnal, active only at twilight and night.

Population. The Spanish lynx is an endangered species. The total population is estimated at approximately 1,200, with only about 100 remaining in Portugal. Their range is scattered, and they are threatened by habitat destruction and by loss of their principal prey, wild rabbits, since many have died from disease.

Distribution. Spain and Portugal.

Felines take care of their fur by grooming meticulously.

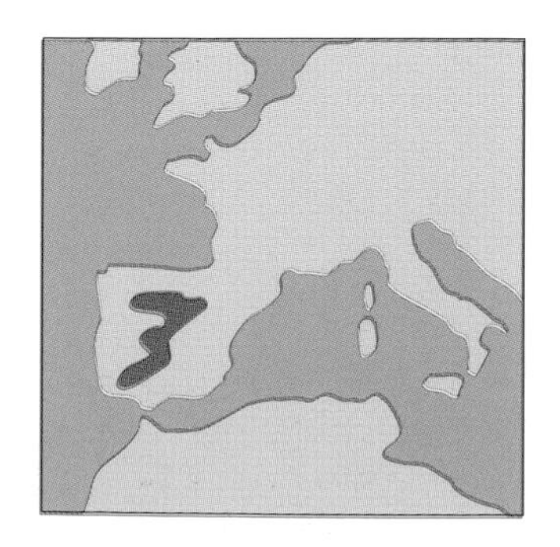

Lynx are territorial. The males defend their domain and signal their presence by scent marking to avoid encounters and, as often as possible, conflicts.

The Bobcat

(Lynx rufus)

Description. The bobcat is close to the North American lynx in appearance, but its legs are shorter and its paws smaller. Its fur is short and dense, and light gray to red in color for the upper part of the body. The stomach is white. Spots or black bands decorate the fur. The back of the ear is black with a white spot. The tail is short, marked with black bands on top and solid white on the underside.

Length. Head and body approximately 24–36 in (62–95 cm); males are slightly larger than females; tail approximately 6 in (14–15 cm).

Weight. Males approximately 22 lb (10 kg); females 15 lb (7 kg); newborns 10–12 oz (280 to 340 g).

Lifespan. Up to 15 years.

Diet. The bobcat primarily eats rabbits and hares, but also deer, rodents, opossums, birds, and snakes.

Reproduction. The bobcat's gestation lasts 50 to 60 days. Usually the young are born between March and June; litters generally consist of four young but can range from one to six. They are weaned at about 8 weeks, and leave their mother the following spring. They reach sexual maturity between one and two years of age.

Lifestyle. The solitary bobcat lives in various habitats. Like the lynx, it is shy and active at twilight or at night. Its territory extends over tens of kilometers and at times overlaps the territory of other individuals.

Population. This species is not threatened but its range is scattered, particularly in the Midwestern and Eastern United States.

Distribution. From southern Canada to central Mexico.

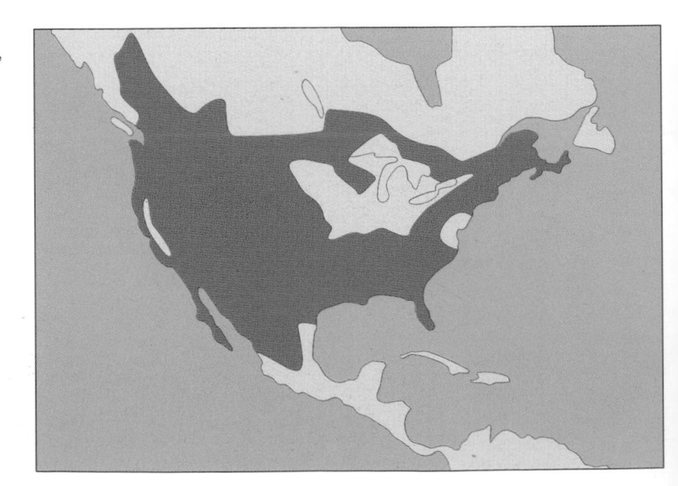

Bobcats are found in a variety of habitats from Canada to Mexico.

The Caracal

(Caracal caracal)

The tufts on the ears accentuate the caracal's facial camouflage. Like most felines, the caracal approaches its prey by crouching in the vegetation. When it reaches a suitable distance, it attacks.

Description. The caracal has a long slender body and long legs, the hind legs longer than the front. Its ears bear black fur tufts. Its tail is one-third to one-half the body length. The cat's dense, short fur is usually reddish-brown with white on the underbelly, but some individuals are completely black.

Length. Head and body length is 24–42 in (60–105 cm); tail 12–14 in (30–35 cm).

Weight. Male approximately 33 lb (15 kg); female 24 lb (11 kg); newborn 10.5 oz (300 g).

Lifespan. Up to 12 years.

Diet. The caracal feeds primarily on rodents, hyrax, dik-diks, antelope young, impalas, reedbucks (*Redunca arundinum*), and on certain species of birds.

Reproduction. The caracal has one or two litters per year; gestation lasts approximately 70 days. It bears litters of one to six young, which open their eyes 9 or 10 days after birth. They begin to eat solid food at around 50 to 70 days and are weaned between 10 and 25 weeks. They remain with their mother about one year, and reach sexual maturity between 1 and 2 years of age.

Lifestyle. The caracal is active at twilight or night and lives in dry wooded areas or dry savannas. It is not found in either desert or tropical environments.

Population. It is not an endangered species.

Distribution. The caracal lives in Africa, a portion of the Middle East, Saudi Arabia, Afghanistan, Pakistan, and northwestern India.

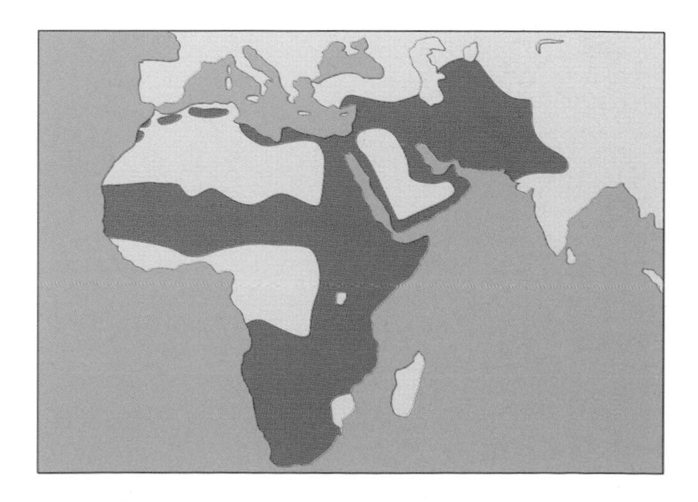

The Serval

(Leptailurus serval)

Description. The serval is a long-legged, slender cat with an elongated head, very large ears, and a short tail. The tawny fur on the back, sides, and legs is decorated with black spots that form bands on the shoulders. The stomach area is white.

Length. Head and body length 27–40 in (67–100 cm); tail 10–18 in (24–45 cm).

Weight. 18–36 lb (8–18 kg).

Lifespan. Usually up to 17 years, although the oldest known serval lived 23 years.

Diet. The serval feeds primarily on rodents, mole rats, birds, lizards, frogs, and insects. It usually hunts on the ground.

Reproduction. Gestation lasts from 66 to 77 days. Generally, the serval bears litters of three young, but litter size can range from one to four. The young begin to eat solid food at around 1 month, and leave their mother at 1 year. They reach sexual maturity between 1 1/2 and 2 years of age.

Lifestyle. The serval lives a solitary life and inhabits prairies where water is present.

Population. The serval is not an endangered species.

Distribution. The serval is found exclusively in Africa. It remains quite abundant south of the Sahara but has definitively disappeared from the north.

Thanks to its large ears, the serval can perceive the slightest noise made by small mammals.

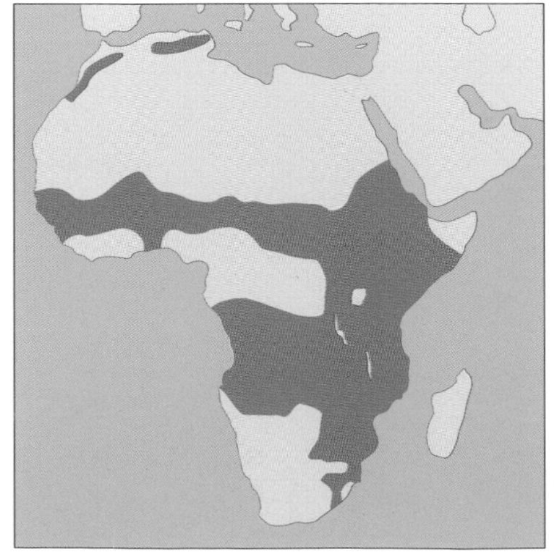

The serval has an unusual gait, different from that of other felines. Its long legs make it an agile jumper and it will leap into the air the way a fox does to pounce on its prey before it has a chance to escape.

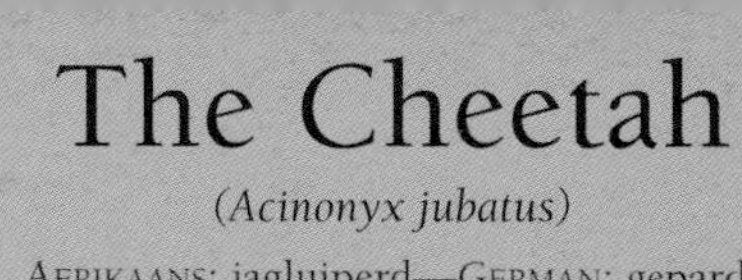

The Cheetah

(Acinonyx jubatus)

AFRIKAANS: jagluiperd—GERMAN: gepard, jagdlopard—SPANISH: guepardo, onza africana—DUTCH: jachtluipard—SWAHILI: duma, msongo—FRENCH: guepard.

Description

The cheetah has a long, svelte body and a broad chest; its legs are long and delicate looking, but strong. Proportionally, its head is small, with wide nostrils and small, round ears. Its claws are not fully retractable; they remain visible in the retracted position. The coat is short and rough, and a short mane covers the nape of the neck and the shoulders. The fur is light tawny to light brown on the back and sides, and whitish on the underbelly; the coat is well covered with small, round black spots. Three to six black rings decorate the tail, which is tipped with white. The fur is lighter in color among individuals from desert areas than those from more humid habitats. The face is marked with two black lines that trace from the inside corner of the eyes to the corners of the mouth. In Zimbabwe, some individuals bear black bands on the torso instead of spots; these cats have been described as a new species, *Ainonyx rex*, but in actuality these cats possess a variant fur type. This variety is referred to as the "royal" or "king" cheetah.

Measurements. Head and body length 45–54 in (112–135 cm); tail length 26–34 in (66–84 cm); height at the withers 30–34 in (75–85 cm); weight 86–143 lb (39–65 kg); newborn weight 9–10 oz (250–280 g).

Locomotion

The cheetah is an excellent runner that can reach 72 mph (120 km/h). With a powerful thrust from its rear legs, the cheetah can reach a speed of 43 mph (72 km/h) within two seconds. As the cat accelerates, all four paws leave the ground. At the moment of landing, the forward paws touch the ground. The powerful shoulder muscles slow the animal after its sprint. The cheetah's anatomy is perfectly adapted to this style of running. The flexibility and musculature of its spinal column function like an arch, which increases running efficiency. The cheetah tires quickly; its sprint cannot be maintained for more than 300 or 400 meters.

Activity

A diurnal (day) hunter, the cheetah usually hunts in the early morning and late afternoon.

Hunting and diet

Cheetahs generally hunt mammals that weigh less than 88 lb (40 kg), including hares, gazelles, jackals, porcupines, impalas, young warthogs, and young antelopes, as well as birds such as guinea fowl, bustards, young ostriches, and so forth. Males hunt alone or in small groups; in the latter case, they can attack larger prey such as wildebeests weighing approximately 176 lb (80 kg). The cheetah hunts by day, sighting its prey from the top of a termite hill or a low branch. It approaches the prey to within thirty or so feet (10 m), and chases it with a sprint lasting from twenty seconds to a maximum of one minute. The cheetah then knocks the prey down and seizes its throat to asphyxiate the

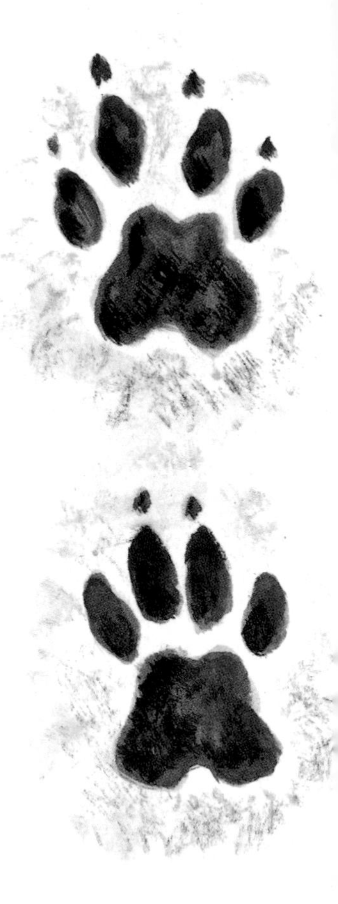

animal. Due to the energy used in this short spurt, pursuits cannot be long or quickly repeated. Needing food with high energy value, the cheetah feeds essentially on the muscle tissue of freshly killed prey; it never eats carcasses. It requires approximately 10 lb (3 kg.) of meat per day; in arid zones, it can reduce its consumption of water and even do without by drinking the urine of its prey and eating desert melons.

Predators

Lions, leopards, African wild dogs, and eagles eat young cheetahs and even at times attack adults.

Social behavior

The social hierarchy of cheetahs is very flexible; the males are solitary or live in groups consisting of two to four related individuals, generally brothers. They mark and defend their territory, which covers approximately 24 sq mi (40 sq km). Territorial conflicts between males are often lethal and create an imbalance in the numbers of males and females, who outnumber the males two to one. However, some males do not possess territory and cover great distances. The females do not seem to have a territory; in the Serengeti (Tanzania), they cover immense distances, up to 480 sq mi (800 sq km), following the migration of Thomson gazelles. These hunting areas are so vast that female cheetahs tolerate but avoid each other. They leave one area when prey becomes scarce and find another hunting area.

Reproduction

For cheetahs, the period of sexual receptivity (called heat or estrus) lasts two days and occurs every seven to ten weeks. No particular reproductive season exists, but

The leopard's anatomy and physiology are perfectly suited to running. This sprinter must eat highly nutritious food in order to attain speeds of up to 72 mph (120 km/h).

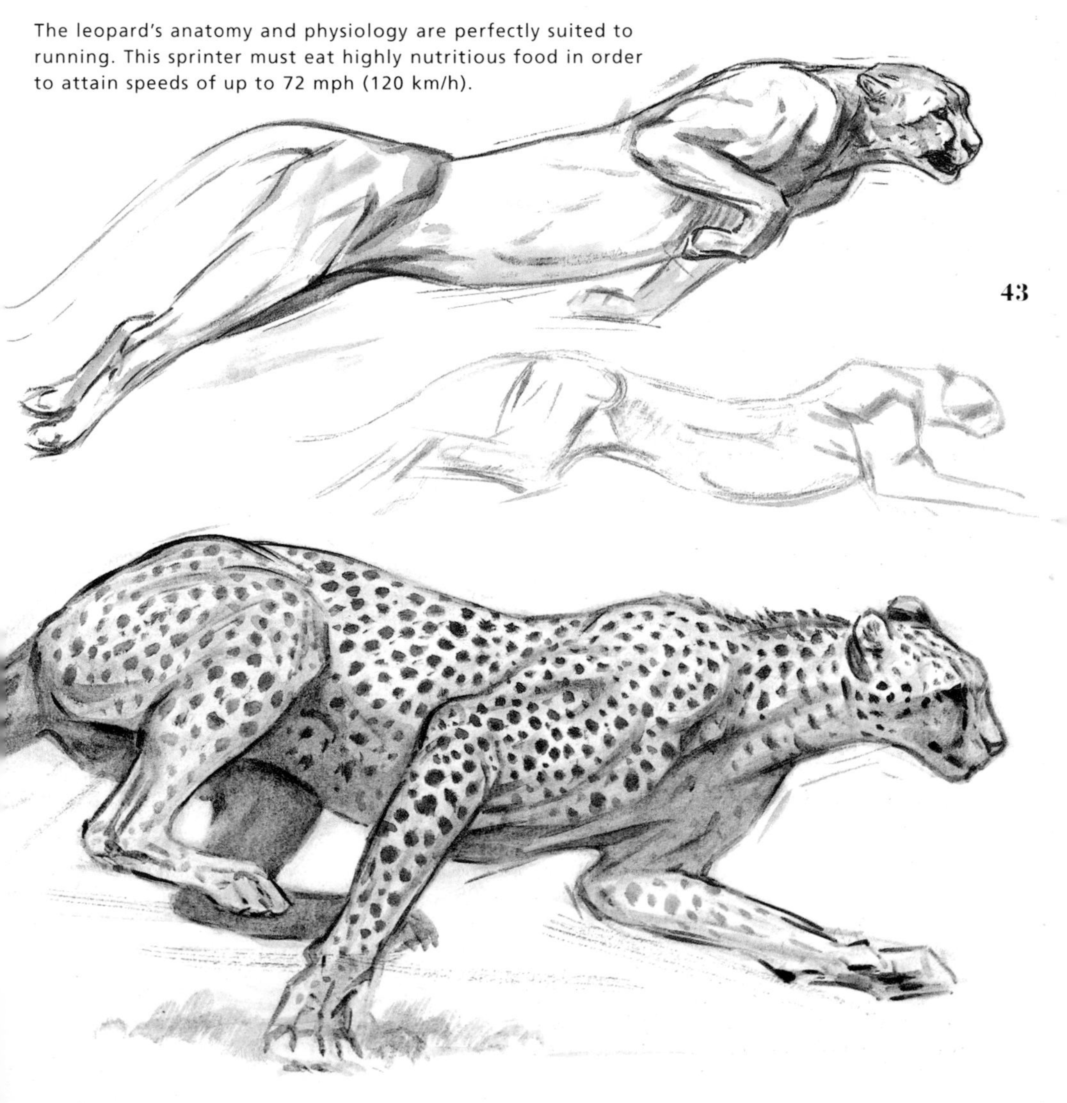

the greatest number of births occurs during gazelle birthing season, which allows the cheetahs to procure prey more easily. Several males compete for the same female, but only one gets the honor of mating with her. Copulation is very brief (under one minute), then the male often remains with the female for several days.

The gestation period is generally 90 to 95 days. Litters include from one to six young, most often two to four. Mortality is very high from birth to 2 months of age; in the Serengeti National park (Tanzania) about 90 percent of young do not reach the age of 3 months due to predators, abandonment by the mother, disease, and so forth. Young have an erect mane that disappears at about 2 1/2 months; until 4 months, their fur is light gray on the back and black on the stomach, which camouflages the young from the numerous predators likely to attack them, including lions, spotted hyenas, and eagles.

Cheetah young open their eyes 10 or 11 days after birth, and begin to eat solid food at 30 to 35 days. Weaning takes place at 12 to 20 weeks. Until 8 months, the young are very playful. Their play provides continuous training for the hunt. When the cubs are about 3 months old, the mother brings live prey and releases it in front of her young to teach them to pursue and kill it. The cubs leave their mother when they are between 14 and 18 months old. Brothers and sisters remain together approximately another 6 months, then the females leave the group. The cubs reach sexual maturity around the age of 20 to 24 months for the females, and two and a half to three years of age for males.

Distribution

Formerly, cheetahs lived outside ombrophile forests throughout Africa and southwest Asia to India; today they remain only in Africa, where they are found in substantial numbers only in Namibia and Kenya. Almost everywhere north of the Sahara, the cheetah has seemingly disappeared. A population exists in Iran (fewer than fifty individuals) and perhaps several specimens survive in Afghanistan and Kazakhstan. Cheetahs can live up to 6,600 ft (2000 m) in altitude.

Status

The cheetah is a vulnerable species. In 1992 its population was estimated at less than 20,000, but other experts estimated at the same time figures of 9,000 to 12,000. Some subspecies are extremely endangered.

According to one theory, at the end of the last ice age approximately 10,000 years ago, at the same time mammoths and saber-tooth tigers disappeared, cheetahs had already nearly become extinct. Out of the numbers that lived at that time in North America, Europe, Asia, and Africa, only a handful survived in regions of Africa and central Asia. This is thought to have caused a genetic bottleneck. In a reduced population, there is an increased chance of two individuals mating that bear the same mutant genes, and thereby the risk of harmful genetic anomalies is greater. On the other hand, when a good genetic mix exists, mutant genes

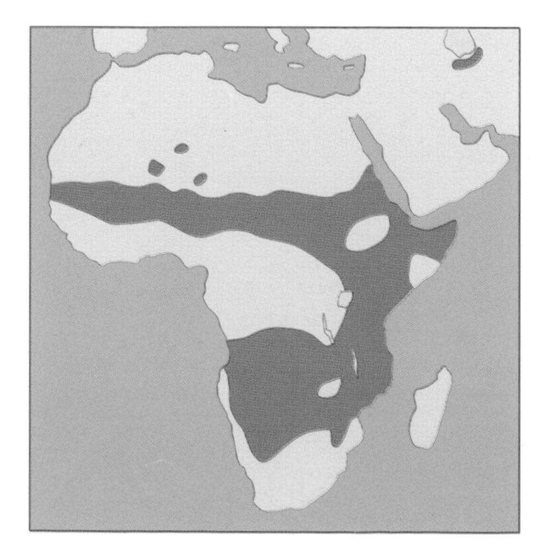

from one parent are masked by the presence of "good" genes from the other. Experiments have shown that the cheetah's genome is ten to a hundred times less variable than the genome of other felines, which can also bring about a greater vulnerability to disease.

Their scattered distribution also limits the healthy mixing of genes; fortunately, the females' travel habits lessen the problem somewhat. This lack of genetic diversity is thought to be one of the reasons why reproduction is so poor among cheetahs in captivity. Because of this theory, one might think that nature has already selected the cheetah for extinction, and that protection efforts for the species are unnecessary because they are bound to fail.

Not so; the reduction in cheetah populations is mostly due to massive hunting and destruction of their prey.

Historical overview

At one time, humans used the cheetah for hunting. Like the falcon, it was blinded by a cowl, then unmasked and released in pursuit of prey. It was used in this manner by the pharaohs of Egypt, emperors of China, Mongols of India, Russian czars, Arab emirs, and the kings of France and England. Reportedly, Akbar the Great, Mongol emperor of India from 1556 to 1605, possessed close to 3,000 cheetahs, but succeeded in producing only one litter.

Later these felines became status symbols and their fur was particularly prized by Hollywood stars. They were captured by the thousands, which greatly reduced their distribution and density. In India, the last three cheetahs in the country were killed in 1947 by the Maharajah of Korwai during a nocturnal hunt. Since mating in captivity was meeting with no success, all the animals were taken from the wild; in general, cheetahs confined to zoos die young and the males have low sperm counts. Cheetahs are severely stressed by forced proximity to other wild animals, particularly in the zoo environment, and this causes successful matings to be rare. In their natural habitat, they are often more numerous in pastoral regions than in protected areas, where too many other large cats are present. In the sixties, however, Dr. Spinelli finally succeeded in getting cheetahs to reproduce by isolating them in his garden.

Termite hills furnish cheetahs with a viewpoint from which to sight prey at a distance, especially during the rainy season when tall grass diminishes visibility. The hills can also serve as a screen during the approach before the final sprint.

Observation Site

Kenya—Tanzania: Masai Mara—Serengeti

The region of Masai Mara and its extension, the Serengeti, the first situated in Kenya and the other in Tanzania, are known for their large herds of wildebeests. Cheetahs are numerous there as well; in 1992, the cheetah population in Kenya was estimated between 1,000 and 1,200. Large ungulates frequent these areas by the thousands and during migration carnivores exploit their weakness and are able to attack them more easily.

The Serengeti park extends to the south by the protected area of the Ngorongoro, where numerous animals also concentrate, living in an enclosed area in the vast crater by the same name.

The Masai Mara park is located in southwest Kenya, 204 mi (340 km) from Nairobi. It is situated at an average altitude of 5,445 ft (1650 m) and covers a surface of 1,002 sq mi (1670 sq km). Founded in 1961, the park is known above all for its migrations of more than a million wildebeests, several hundreds of thousands of zebras and buffalo, and numerous antelope and gazelles, who come from the Serengeti in July and August. The park is irrigated by the tree-lined Mara river, and by the Talek. The animals particularly gather in its western portion, bordered by the Oloololo escarpment. Tourists are numerous in the eastern section of the park, near the Oloololo and Talek entrances. The film *Out of Africa* (Sydney Pollack) was filmed in the park with its magnificent panoramas. The film is based on the book by Karen Blixen, who lived in this region of Kenya for many years.

The Serengeti, or "vast plain" in the Masai language, is the oldest and largest park in Tanzania. It extends for 8,858 sq mi (14,763 sq km). This immense plain, to the northwest of the country, extends the Masai Mara. It is strewn with large granite outcroppings (called *kopjes*) and covered with forest areas and treed savannas. Just as in the Masai Mara, the concentration of fauna is enormous. From November to May,

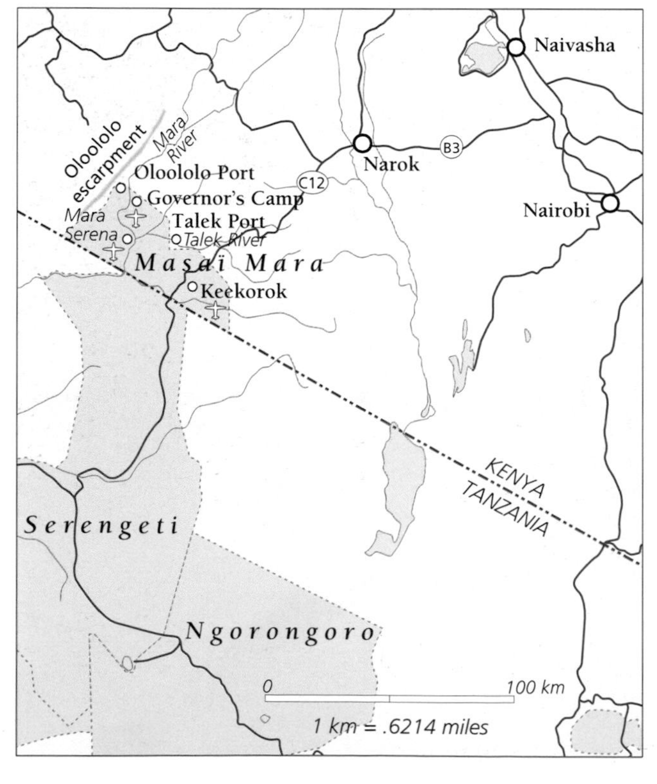

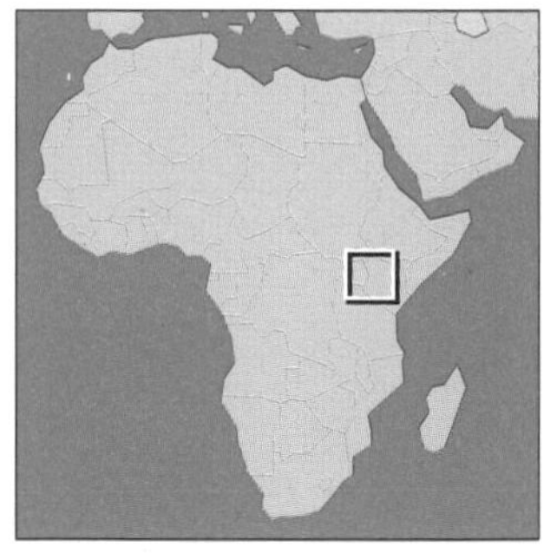

during the rainy season, grass is abundant. At the first signs of dryness, the animals move toward the wooded regions and brushy savannas. Then, when grass becomes rarer still, the great herds move toward the west of the plains and return north to the Masai Mara where the vegetation persists and where the water sources are permanent. In November, when the rains return, they make a half-turn and leave again for the fertile volcanic soil of the upper plateaus of the Ngorongoro.

Fauna and flora

This is a region of savannas and grassy plains, punctuated by parasol acacia trees. Aside from the large numbers of wildebeests present during the migrations, one can observe warthogs, zebras, black rhinoceroses, elephants, buffalo, Masai giraffes, Thomson gazelles, Grant gazelles, impalas, topis, hartebeest, and baboons. Other large cats are also visible, such as leopards lounging on the rocks or the branches, and lions resting in the shade of a cluster of acacias. The other

Ibises are among the rich bird life of this region.

Large herds of zebras and gazelles graze in the Ngorongoro crater.

The Masai

In the eyes of the general public, the Masai people represent this region of Africa. They are nomadic warriors present everywhere in Kenya, moving with their cattle from one pasture land to another. They speak Maa, from which their name is derived. They are particularly dedicated to their traditions, and some Masai reject any modern innovations.

Their history is not well known. We know that they are the product of a mingling between the Nilotic- and Cushitic-speaking peoples approximately 1,000 years ago in the region of Lake Turkana. They lived there until the fifteenth century, then slowly moved southward, where they forged a reputation for being powerful warriors. At the beginning of the colonial period, the Masai cooperated with the English and offered only slight resistance to the increasing number of colonists and the taking of their pasture lands. At that time, almost 90 percent of their cattle was decimated by bovine plague and drought. When conflicts broke out among previously united populations, the Masai were displaced to a previously uncultivated savanna in southern Kenya, the location of the current Masai Mara, and within several decades lost almost all their pasture lands. The Kikuyus bought large tracts of land that they turned into agricultural areas, which also affected the Masai lifestyle. Beginning in the 1960s, the creation of the preserve, the growth of the population, and the increase in cattle leasing have brought about constant pressures.

Today, conflicts with authorities are frequent, even more so because the Masai do not understand land boundaries; they are not farmers, and the notion of land ownership is foreign to them, so they have not accepted settlement plans.

According to Masai oral tradition, Maa gave birth to both the Masai and the Somalis, whose ancestors were called Parakwos. These Parakwos, the gods' chosen people, were said to have received cattle as a gift from the gods. It is for this reason that the Masai believe that those who own cattle and are not Masai have stolen it from them. Current law in Kenya prevents them from "recovering" their "stolen" assets, cattle being most precious to them. The Masai are nourished essentially on the blood of their animals (taken directly from the jugular vein) in the form of blood sausage, and on their animals' milk (fresh or curdled, and stored in long, decorated gourds). They also eat millet and maize, and consume mutton and goat, rarely eating the meat of their cattle or of wild animals. They live in round huts made of branches, mud, and dung, called *bomas,* which they surround with a thorn fence to protect themselves from wild animals. When they move, they abandon their dwellings and transport their belongings on the backs of donkeys.

Boys and girls of the same age are grouped in an ensemble of huts called *manyatta.* For men, age and clan have great importance. After childhood, young men from 14 to 18 years of age are circumcised. They then become warriors, or *morans,* and must respect certain taboos, such as not touching alcohol, and take on the duty of keeping the cattle and protecting the clan. They carry lances and shields decorated with black, red, and white to display their status. To prove their courage, they must have killed a lion with only their lance.

They take care of their appearance, most particularly their long hair braids, and decorate themselves with jewelry. Seven or eight years after their initiation, they marry, cut their hair and, after a ceremony called *eunoto,* become members of the community of elders. They then participate in meetings and make decisions concerning the clan.

A Masai girl becomes a woman through female circumcision and marriage. She shaves her head and wears long leather earrings. It is her responsibility to make household items and build the house.

Today, these rituals are disappearing. Some Masai benefit from tourism by selling their handcrafted items. The Masai have the right to allow their herds to graze in the Masai Mara park with the exception of a totally protected area of 193 sq mi (500 sq km).

principal carnivores of the Masai Mara and the Serengeti are the spotted hyena, the African wild dog, and the jackal. The rivers shelter numerous crocodiles and hippopotami. In this region also live approximately 450 species of birds, including vultures, marabou storks, ostriches, bustards, hornbills, and also the migratory birds of Europe and Asia such as storks, kestrel falcons, buzzards, swallows, swifts, and so on.

Observation

Observing the wildlife of the Masai Mara or the Serengeti is done in all-terrain vehicles, preferably early in the morning or at the end of the day. The best season is July to October or in January and February. Numerous organized safaris exist, which can be reserved before your arrival or in Nairobi. It is also possible to rent a car for a personal safari (the road network is reliable); if you do, it's advisable to purchase road maps before you leave. Advance reservations are a must in peak season (December to March). An entry fee is charged at the entrance to the Masai Mara park; one cannot travel through the park on foot, and traffic is forbidden from 7 P.M. to dawn. On the other hand, it is possible to fly over the park in hot air balloon (leaving from Keekorok, from Mara Serena, and from Governor's Camp). You can also choose to take a three-to-five hour guided hike led by Masai guides. Avoid visits in minibuses, and, of course, do not chase the animals.

Wild animals can be located by watching the vultures in search of carcasses. Monkeys clamoring in the trees can also signal the presence of a cat. Approach slowly and keep your distance; you should come equipped with binoculars or with a spotting scope. Cheetahs are known to be nonaggressive, but caution is necessary, notably because of the presence of other large predators in the area. Cheetahs can also be observed in Kenya in the other principal preserves (the Nairobi and Samburu parks, for example).

PRACTICAL INFORMATION

The best period for observation is from July to October or in January and February.

TRANSPORTATION

■ **BY PLANE.** Eight-hour flights link Paris and Nairobi. Commuter flights between Nairobi and Masai Mara run twice a day.

In Tanzania, the main airports are Dar es-Salaam (Paris to Dar es-Salaam takes 11 hours), Kilimanjaro, and Zanzibar.

■ **BY CAR.** From Nairobi allow five to ten hours driving time. In Nairobi take the route to Naivasha, then go toward Narok. After Narok, an all-terrain vehicle is absolutely necessary to reach the Masai Mara. Remember to fill up with gas in Narok.

CLIMATE

Kenya. Maximum temperatures: 70°–79° F (21°–26° C); minimum 48°–57° F (9°–14° C). Monthly precipitation: heavy in April and May, 6 in and 8 in (155 mm and 190 mm); November and December, 8 in and 5 in (190 mm and 115 mm); light in July and August, less than an in (17 and 20 mm/month). There are ten hours of sunlight a day in February and only 4 hours in July–August.

Tanzania. Maximum temperatures: 82°–84° F (28°–29° C); minimum: 63°–66° F (17°–19° C), cooler in the Ngorongoro: 45°–63° F (7°–17° C). Monthly rainfall heavy from November to April: up to 6 in (160 mm) and light (less than an inch; 15 mm) from June to August. There are 11 hours of sunlight a day in July and only 7 hours from December to April.

LODGING

Lodges or canvas camps are available in or outside the park. The camping area in Oloolaimutia is run by the Masai; another is situated along the Talek river, near the Talek entrance, and a third near the Oloololo entrance. Make advance reservations in Nairobi.

VISITS

It is possible to visit a Masai village, near the Oloololo entrance. Visit in the morning when there are few tourists, as this allows better contact with the Masai.

RECOMMENDATIONS

Take insect repellent.
Be careful of tourist overcrowding, particularly during July and August.

Observation site

Namibia: Etosha National Park

The region is situated around the former salt lake of Etosha. A large portion, the Etosha Pan, is completely flooded during the November to April rainy season. When the water recedes, the grasses grow back and the black-tailed wildebeest, the springbok, and the zebra move in to graze. This shallow basin is bordered by thickets of mopan. These shrubs, capable of resisting the region's high temperatures, constitute 80 percent of Etosha's vegetation. According to a Bushman legend, God had succeeded in finding a place on earth for all animals and all plants except for one, the *Moringa ovalifolia,* or mopan. He decided to throw these shrubs into the air so chance might decide their location; they all fell to the ground at Etosha, where they have formed ever since the haunted mopan forest. Created in 1907, the Etosha preserve is the largest animal preserve in Africa, covering some 7,596 sq mi (22,270 sq km). It is bordered by two rivers, the Kunene and the Okavango. The park is entirely enclosed, preventing the animals from migrating and necessitating complete management of the fauna.

Fauna and flora

This region shelters a population of cheetahs, as well as 114 species of mammals including warthogs, giraffes, duikers, Kirk's dik-diks, black-tailed wildebeest, springboks, Burchell zebras, Hartmann zebras, great kudus, Cap elands, hartebeest, roan antelope, and impalas. The carnivores of Etosha are notably lions, leopards, caracals, aardwolves, spotted hyenas, tawny mongooses, and ratels. The park shelters 340 species of birds, one-third of which are migratory. Numerous pink flamingos frequent Fisher's Pan, and some 35 species of bird of prey. The flora consists largely of mopanes. The other

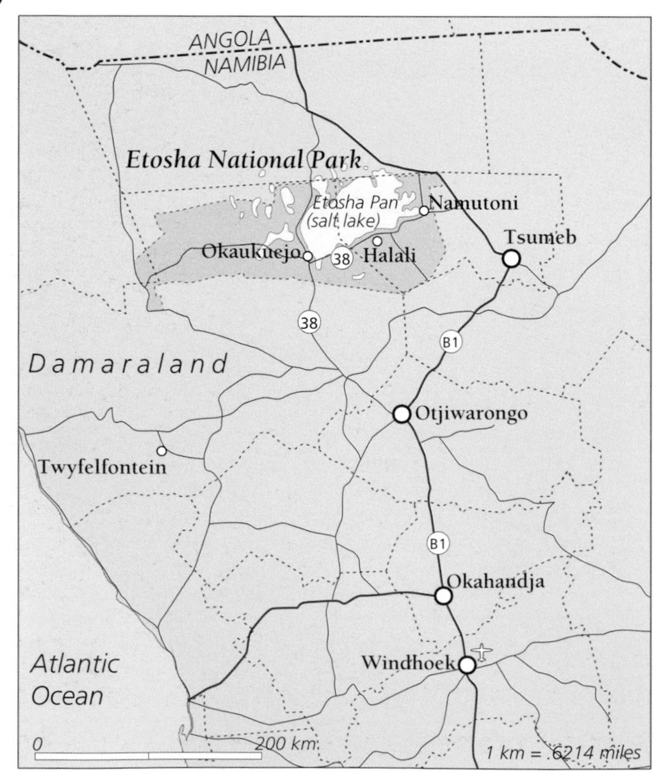

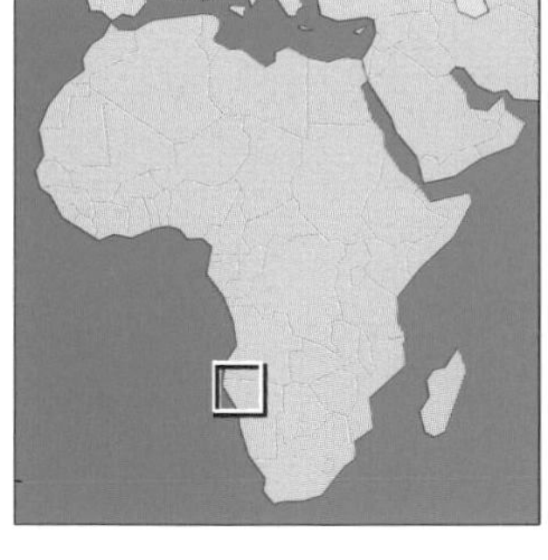

The great kudu is one of the inhabitants of Etosha park, among the hundred or so mammals that can be found there.

After the rainy season, Etosha Pan becomes a vast prairie of grasses grazed on by ungulates like the springboks seen here.

very frequently found plants are parasol acacias and *euphorbias* such as wartwort.

Observation

The dry season, between April and September, is best for observation. The herds gather around watering areas (some 30 of them, situated especially in the eastern portion of the park); the lions and cheetahs can be seen, particularly around the Klein and Groot Okeviu (to the north of Namutoni), Goas (to the northeast of Halali), Aroe (east of Namutoni) and Rietfontein (to the west of Halali). Cheetahs and other animals are viewed from an enclosed all-terrain vehicle, preferably early in the morning or in the evening. Observation is also possible during the day; however, visits on foot are impossible. At the Okaukuejo, lights allow the animals to be seen at night, which is especially interesting in the case of lions and other nocturnal predators. Wild animals, particularly cheetahs, often can be successfully viewed outside the park.

The cheetah eats only freshly killed prey.

A number of large mammals, among them elephants, live in the Etosha park.

The Bushmen

After having lived several millennia on the plains of Tanzania, Ethiopia, Uganda, and southern Sudan, the Bushmen, between the twelfth and fifteenth centuries, were chased into the desert. Since that time, they have been confined to eastern Namibia and the Kalahari desert in Botswana.

They are nomads, but at times are sedentary. They are known for their small stature, light skin, salient cheekbones, and almond eyes. Their features, similar to those of Asians, are an enigma for ethnologists, but the theory of Asiatic origin has finally been excluded. The women have unique, well-developed buttocks where fat is stored, which was certainly an adaptation from periods of famine.

The Bushmen live in groups of 25 to 60, without laws or hierarchy. The men hunt with javelins and arrows coated with a poison made from the larvae of scarab beetles and tree sap. The women are responsible for gathering, and for the construction of grass-roofed branch huts as resting places during nighttime stops. With straws, Bushmen draw up water from underground layers or water contained in tree branches, then conserve the water in ostrich egg shells. They play music with mouth arcs, lyres with four strings, and mite cocoons filled with seeds and pebbles. During ritual ceremonies the women dance, clap their hands and sing, and invoke symbolic animals like the giraffe or the Cape eland; the men stomp their feet and imitate animal sounds. Healers go into trances to reach the spirit world and to obtain the power to care for the sick and resolve conflicts and the like. During the full moon, the Bushmen gather around a tree for the purification dance. The women sit in a circle and sing while the men dance. The shaman jumps into the circle. He touches the women, and blows into their mouths, ears, and navels.

PRACTICAL INFORMATION

The Etosha preserve is closed from November to the end of March.

TRANSPORTATION

■ **BY PLANE.** Regular flights run between Paris and Windhoek (15 hours, with stopover). From Windhoek take the flight to Etosha.

■ **BY CAR.** It is possible to rent a car in Windhoek. To reach Etosha, you must take the northern route toward Okahandja, Otjiwarongo, then for Tsumeb (Route B1), then take route C35 to Namutoni. The distance from Windhoek to Etosha is 344 mi (553 km).

CLIMATE

Temperatures: maximum 77°–93° F (25°–34° C), above 86° F (30°C) from September to May; minimum from 63° F (17°C) (May–August) to 64° F (18°C). Monthly rainfall: heavy from December to January, heaviest in January and February, 5–6 in (124–140 mm), light from May to October—up to an inch. There are six to 11 hours of sun per day, with the most between July and September.

LODGING

Three camps for visitors exist in the eastern portion of the park: Namutoni, Halali, and Okaukuejo (with a watering spot which is lit at night). The stay is limited to three nights. It is necessary to make reservations with the Director of Tourism, Private Bag 13267, Windhoek. Camping is forbidden in the park.

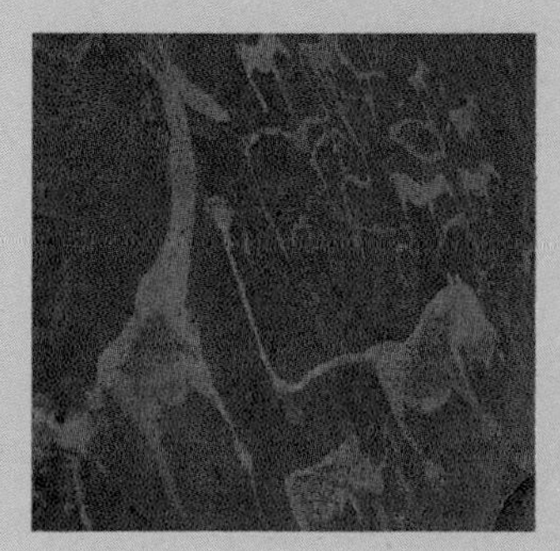

VISITS

In Damaraland, Twyfelfontein, you can visit a site with a collection of 2,000 rupestral drawings made by the Khoi-khois 3,000 years ago, among which is a fresco of cheetahs chasing ostriches. Other paintings depict scenes of dance and mythological scenes of humans with the heads of animals. The artists painted with the blood of cape elands, sacrificed for the occasion. Healers danced in front of the paintings, so that the blood would transmit spiritual powers to them.

To reach Twyfelfontein, from Tsumeb take Route B1 toward the south to Otjiwarongo, then continue via Route 38 in the direction of Outjo, then take Route 39 and fork to the left.

RECOMMENDATIONS

Plan on bringing a wool coat for the evenings and insect repellent. Walking through the park is forbidden.

The Lion

(Panthera leo)

Afrikaans : leeu — German : löwe
Dutch : leeuw — Spanish : león
French : lion — Swahili : simba

Description

The lion possesses a massive body and a broad head, short, rounded ears with a black spot on its dorsal side, long massive legs, and a long tail. Its coat is solid and light brown to deep ocher. At times white lions occur, but they are not albinos. The cubs have spotted fur, and when grown the spots sometimes remain on the legs and stomach. The males have a magnificent mane that darkens and develops with age; the color varies according to geographic origin. This mane protects the male from the claws and fangs of an adversary during combats. Also, it serves to make the lion appear bigger and more impressive and vigorous than he actually is. However, it makes males too easily seen to hunt prey. The tail, used to swat flies, ends in a black tuft that hides a horned spur.

Measurements. Male: head and body length 70–100 in (170–250 cm); tail 36–42 in (90–105 cm); height 49 in (123 cm); weight 330–550 lb (150–250 kg). Female: head and body length 56–70 in (140–175 cm); tail 28–40 in (70–100 cm); height 43 in (107 cm); weight 264–400 lb (120–182 kg). Newborn: 2.6–3 lb (1.2–1.4 kg).

Lifespan. Generally, lions live 13 to 15 years but can live 30 years in captivity. The females sometimes reach 16 years of age, but the males do not live as long—not longer than 12 years—and are excluded from groups when they are too old. They have difficulty feeding themselves on their own and cannot easily defend themselves

The lionesses hunt for the pride. They circle the prey together, increasing the chances of a successful hunt.

from groups of young males. The lionesses hunt for the pride. They circle the prey together, increasing the chances of a successful hunt.

Locomotion

The lion is a good runner and can reach 40 mph (65 km/h). It is capable of climbing and swims well.

Activity

Lionesses hunt most often at night. Lions can be active by day if they are not disturbed, but their hunt is less efficient. They appear to sleep constantly, but in fact, they sleep during the day and are active at night. All the same, they sleep from 16 to 20 hours a day.

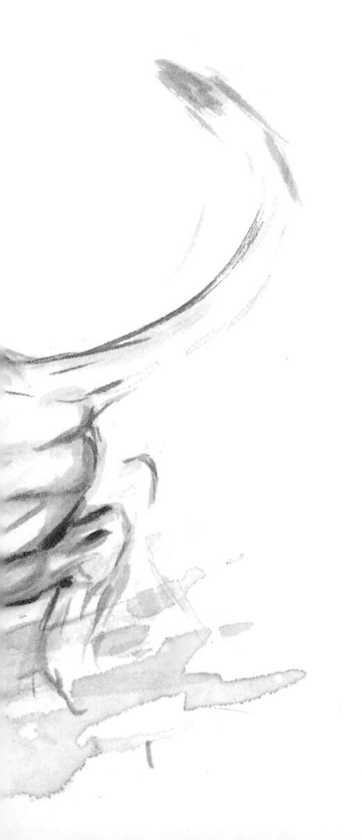

Hunting and diet

The lion's prey is varied and includes giraffes, buffalo, zebras, antelopes, gazelles, wildebeests, and warthogs, but also hippopotami, small rhinoceroses, and elephants, which can be dangerous. At times, lions feed on small mammals, birds, snakes, and crocodiles. They compete for prey with leopards, cheetahs, African wild dogs, and hyenas, but those groups feed more on prey weighing no more than 220 lb (100 kg), whereas lions regularly attack animals of about 550 lb (250 kg). In addition, cases of cannibalism are known, especially of the young. Lions, especially males, also feed on carcasses. They spot the carcasses by the flight of vultures and the cries of hyenas. In the Ngorongoro, 84 percent of the carcasses eaten by lions had been killed by hyenas. Lions steal the prey of cheetahs and leopards as well.

Most hunting is done by the female, alone or in a group. When hunting in a group, they spot the prey and circle it, crouching, then move forward to a distance of about 100 ft (30 m). The nearest female leaps on the prey, knocks it to the ground, and kills it by biting the nape of the neck or the throat, by breaking its backbone, or by holding the muzzle closed and suffocating it. One charge out of five brings success; the prey is faster than the lionesses but the latter's hunting technique compensates for the handicap. The males of the pride eat first, then the females. The cubs are last and they have been known to die of hunger when game is rare. An adult lion needs about 11 lb (5 kg) (for a female) to about 16 lb (7 kg) (for a male) of meat a day and it can ingest 77 lb (35 kg) in one eating. Lions drink water daily but can do without for several months during a dry period.

Predators

Hyenas and African wild dogs attack adult lions. Lion cubs are the prey of hyenas, leopards, and pythons.

Social behavior

Lions are the only cats to have true social organization. They live in a pride of from 3 to 40 individuals (15 on average), organized around a stable core of related lionesses (up to 15 adult females). Generally, the females do not accept lions with which they are not familiar. They favor their own litter, but participate equally in the protection and feeding of the pride's other cubs; young orphans are adopted by the females of the pride.

Young females remain in the pride, while males leave it as soon as they are mature, wandering until they find a new pride. Since they are inexperienced, the young males often associate with others for hunting and defense. These alliances of related or unrelated males can last several years. Such a group can join a pride of lions by chasing away the male residents. The size and the darkness of the mane are signs of development and maturity; younger individuals with less developed and lighter-colored manes will avoid lions with well-developed manes. Male lions also leave a pride to search for other females. The lionesses who remain with the pride do not accept just any new male; they generally accept the most powerful. The arrival of new males often means massacres: they kill the cubs, the young, and the adult females who refuse to mate with them. For this reason females that have cubs often flee at the arrival of new males. The females who remain whose cubs are killed are quickly sexually receptive again. The newly introduced males will assure their own lineage to the detriment of the previous males.

Territory is marked by roaring, audible from 20 mi, (8 km) and spraying urine. The territory is defended against outside lions by the entire adult pride, but especially by the males whose size and power more effectively discourage any aggressors. While extending their territory, large prides have a tendency to divide into subgroups. Territorial dimensions vary, acccording to the size of the pride and the landscape, from 12–240 sq mi (20–400 sq km.)

Play fighting allows young lions to learn to capture prey or escape from predators, and to test their speed and agility. These games prepares them for their future interactions with other animals.

Reproduction

Lions have no reproductive season. The females come into heat every three months for four to eight days. An adult male remains with the female in estrus and couples with her several times over several days. When new males are introduced into the pride, numerous periods of mating precede a first fertilization, allowing them to "choose" the females who will be reproductive.

Gestation lasts in general from 102 to 113 days—short for such a large animal. Often several females in the pride will give birth to their cubs at the same time; this simultaneity aids adoption in case a mother dies. The female gives birth concealed in a thicket or rock grouping. The litter consists of from one to six cubs (most often two or three); the newborn cubs weigh from 2–4 lb (1–1.75 kg) (less than 1 percent of an adult's weight). The newborn's body measures 9 in (22 cm), and the tail adds another 3 in (8 cm). The cubs' fur is spotted. Their eyes are closed, and open within one to nine days. The cubs begin to move about at 3 weeks, and run at 6 weeks. At 8 weeks, they begin to eat meat but are not completely weaned until about 6 months.

Mortality among cubs is high, as high as 80 percent in young up to 2 years of age. The young accompany the adults to the hunt starting at 14 weeks, but begin to hunt alone around the age of 2 years. Lion cubs are grown at 18 months but do not really mature until they are 5 or 6 years old. Their mane begins to grow at 18 months. Young males are chased from the pride when they are two and a half to three years of age; they leave as a group and eventually challenge the males of a pride in order to take their places; the battles can be violent and at times lethal.

Distribution

The lion lives in open country, in savannas and semideserts, and in the mountains, up to altitudes of 14,850 ft (4,500 m). It does not inhabit dense forests. It is found in Africa between the 20th parallel North and the 23rd parallel South, in Natal in South Africa to the 27th parallel South, and in northwestern India in the Gir Forest.

Status

The Asian lion has practically disappeared; only some 300 remain in the Gir Forest in India. In Africa, it is also an endangered species, with certain subspecies on the path to extinction.

Historical overview

During the Pleistocene era (1.8 million to 10,000 years ago), the lion inhabited Africa, Asia Minor, Arabia, India, Ceylon, Europe, North America, and the central and northwestern portions of South America. Rupestral engravings confirm its existence in Europe 15,000 years ago. At this time, the lion was still found in all of Africa, the Mediterranean basin, the Middle East, and India. During the fourth century B.C., Aristotle noted its presence in Greece. The Romans used lions from North Africa and Asia Minor a great deal for their circuses. Lions still populated the Near East in the Middle Ages and the Middle East and northern India during the last century.

Lions would have been totally exterminated from Asia if, at the beginning of the century, the nabab of Junagadh had not made the decision to protect the few remaining in the Gir Forest. In 1913, no more than 20 remained in that region; today, thanks to protection measures, they number approximately 300.

Lion populations are scattered through all of Africa because of intensive hunting, eradication of their prey, and destruction of their natural environment.

In the Ngorongoro crater in Tanzania, confinement and inbreeding have brought about a lack of genetic diversity and a decrease in their resistance to disease; a portion of the lions in this region was decimated by an outbreak of disease.

In the Etosha park in Namibia, the situation is the reverse: the enclosed nature of the park has brought about a proliferation of lions and a decrease of other predators. In 1981, a contraceptive pill was tried on five test groups living near Okaukuejo. The lionesses were immobilized and examined, then a contraceptive was administered to them. This experiment was a success; no side effects were noted after the contraception was stopped and the lionesses once more were able to give birth to healthy young. Nevertheless, it is regrettable that such procedures are necessary for the management of the wildlife in this preserve; the fact that the park is a closed environment has also caused epidemics and prevented migration.

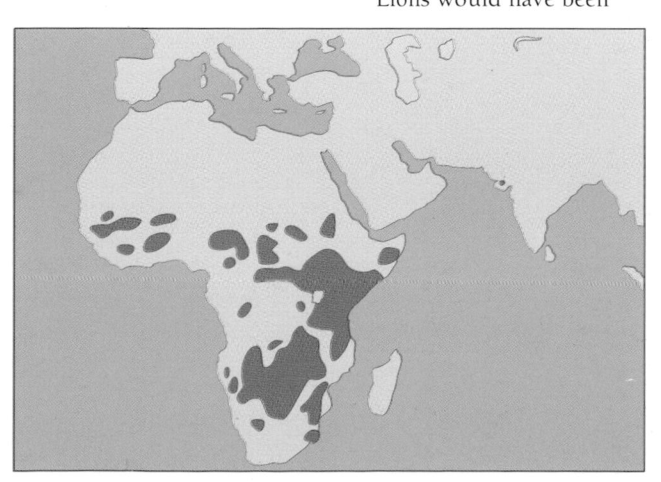

Observation site

India (Gujarat): The Gir Forest

In India, the lion is a symbol of nobility, power, and justice. It is also represented as the steed of the goddess Durga. Despite what they represent here as in the rest of Asia, lions survive in India only in an area of several hundred square kilometers in the Gujarat region. At the beginning of the twentieth century, following an invitation to hunt lions which the nabab of Junagadh had extended to Lord Curzon, the Indian viceroy, the inhabitants of the district reacted strongly to the threat of extermination of the last Asian lions. The Viceroy canceled the hunt and advised the nabab of Junagadh to protect these last specimens. When Sasan Gir Lion Sanctuary, the national park of Sasan Gir, was created to protect the last Asian lions and their habitat, only about twenty remained.

Sasan Gir Lion Sanctuary consists of 840 sq mi (1,400 sq km) in a wooded oasis in the middle of the desert. In 1980, it sheltered 200 lions; the number today is estimated at close to 300 (284 in 1994). The creation of the park caused cattle ranchers (*maldharis*) to lose the lands on which their cattle grazed. Needless to say, when lions leave the preserve and kill cattle, especially calves, the local populations are rather hostile about the preserve. Some, however, benefit from the tourism linked to the presence of these magnificent wild animals.

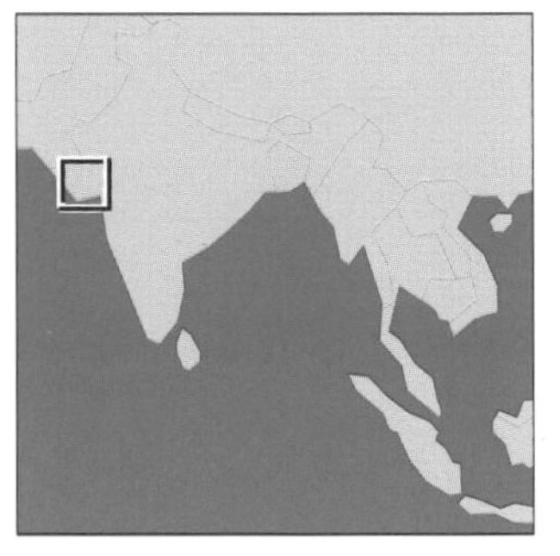

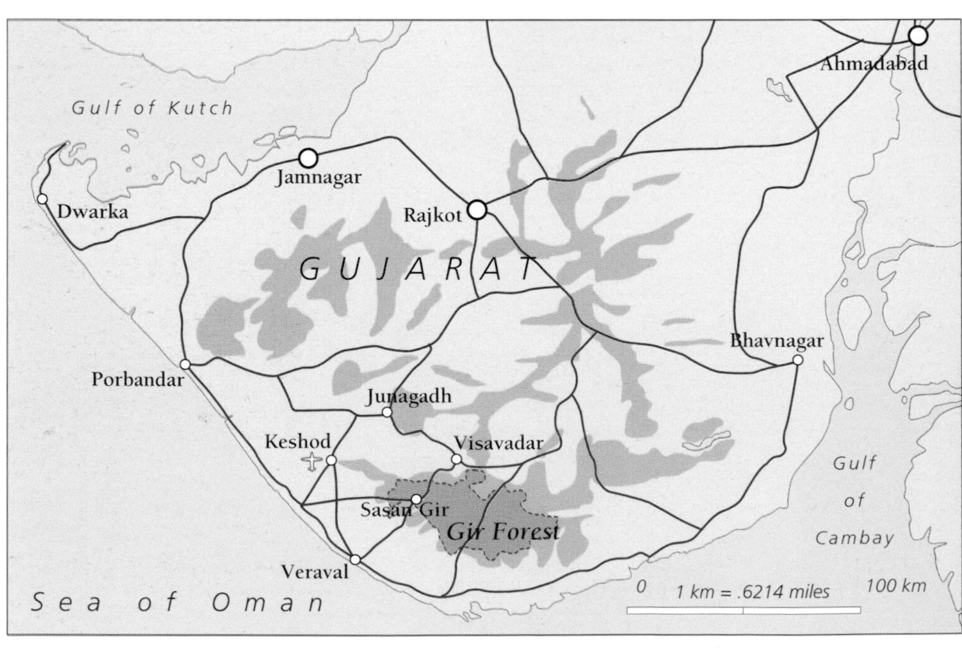

The four-horned antelope (*Tetracerus quadricornis*) exists only in India.

Fauna and flora

Sasan Gir Lion Sanctuary, the last refuge for the Asian lion, is also rich in other mammals such as the sloth bear, hyenas, leopards, foxes, wolves, nilghai antelopes, Chinkara gazelles, sambars, chitals, muntjacs, wild boars, and various species of monkeys. You can also find the four-horned antelope (*Tetracerus quadricornis*), which exists only in India. Lake Kamaleshwar and the multiple rivers of the surrounding area shelter crocodiles. In addition, there is a crocodile hatchery at Sasan Gir.

Many bird species also inhabit this region: parrots, parakeets, loricules, woodpeckers, fishing martins, and numerous species of wild gallinaces, among them blue peacocks and various pheasants in shimmering colors.

The forest includes a wide variety of plant species (trees, shrubs, and brush).

Related lionesses form the stable core of the pride. Young orphans can be raised by an adoptive mother.

Observation

The best time of year to visit the Gir Forest is between January and April; you should completely avoid the monsoon season, May to September. This won't be hard, since the park is closed during that time (mid-May to mid-October). Lions can be observed in the evening and at night, but the best time is always morning. "Lion shows" are organized so tourists can get close to them. Previously, park personnel attracted lions with either dead or live tethered cattle. Park personnel took this opportunity to identify and count the lions, and sometimes care for them. Tourists could be present for the event. Today, the lions can be observed around watering areas instead; this way, the lions can be observed behaving normally.

To visit the preserve, you must get permission from the office of the Sinh Sadan Forest Lodge at Sasan Gir; the permit is valid for three days.

It is advisable to travel by jeep rather than minibus. Three trails lead approximately 15 to 21 mi (25–35 km) into the park. Guided safaris are conducted every day, 7:00 to 10:00 A.M. and 2:00 to 6:30 P.M. Advance reservations are required. For safety reasons, the safaris are led by a forest guide; lions are often found in prides of eight to ten and can be dangerous. All-terrain vehicles with removable tops seating six are used for the tours. The price of the tour depends on the size of the group, and a tip should be taken into account, as well as an additional charge for photographic equipment.

The lion's mane is a means of communication between male lions. It also indicates the lion's state of health, and protects it during combat.

The lions in the Gir barely number 300. They are the sole survivors of the Asiatic lions that once populated a large part of the continent.

The lion in Western and Eastern civilization

Lions have always been important symbols of power, related to the sun, good and evil, and life and death. Representations of them have been found dating to the paleolithic era. In Mesopotamia, the lion was likened to Ishtar, the goddess of love and war.

According to Greek mythology, the lion was created by Apollo; his sister Diana made its miniature copy, the cat, in order to ridicule her brother. In Rome, lions accompanied emperors in their triumphs; they were used in the circuses, particularly at the time of the martyring of the Christians.

In medieval Europe, the lion symbolized the resurrection of Christ; in those days people believed lion cubs died just after birth and three days later their fathers came to give life back to them. Many knights in the Middle Ages chose the lion as the emblem on their coat of arms. In India, lions were associated with the rising sun. For Buddhists, the lion is sacred, and is considered the defender of the law and of religious monuments.

In many civilizations, killing a lion constituted proof of courage, and the hunt was reserved for sovereigns.

Lions also have an important place in art; they were portrayed as symbols of strength, the images of which were borrowed notably from Greek mythology (the first of Hercules' works was to kill the lion of Nemea), or served to represent "savagery" and instinct (as opposed to civilization). Although not native to the country, the lion appeared in Chinese art from the first century A.D. Lions, albeit rare, were known there because they were given as gifts by foreign sovereigns or used in trade. For example, the Romans traded lions for Chinese silk. Lions are very often used in Buddhist art, and depictions of lions decorate the entries of numerous buildings to serve as guardians. These sculptures are so stylized that Westerners believed them to be Pekingese dogs.

PRACTICAL INFORMATION

The best time to visit the Gir Forest is between January and April.

TRANSPORTATION

BY PLANE. Regular flights link Paris and Bombay. Daily flights link Bombay to Keshod, situated 24 mi (40 km) from Junagadh and 52 mi (86 km) from Sasan Gir.

BY CAR. The preserve is located 32 mi (54 km) from Junagadh, by way of Visavadar.

BY BUS OR TRAIN. You can also reach the Gir Forest by state bus or steam train. Sasan Gir is situated on the western railway line. You can also reach it on the Junagadh bus line.

CLIMATE

Temperatures: maximum 84°–88° F (29°–31° C) (December–February) to 104°–108°F (40°–42° C) (April–May); minimum 57°–59° F (14°–15° C) (December–January) to 81° F (27°C) (May–July). The monsoon season begins at the end of May. Monthly rainfall: maximum July to September, 7–13 in (165–315 mm) and minimum (less than an inch; 0–13 mm) from October to May. There are 4 to 5 hours of sunlight per day in July and August, and 10 to 11 hours from October to May.

LODGING

Two hotels can be found in the village of Sasan Gir. The Sinh Sadan Forest Lodge is a ten-minute walk from the train station. A reservation is required. The other, the Lion Safari Lodge of the State Corporation of Gujarat, is situated near the river.

VISITS

West of Gujarat, in the city of Dvarka 82 mi (137 km) west of Jamnagar, said to be founded by Krishna himself, is the Hindu temple of Dvarkadish. Above the entrance is a depiction of the elephant god Ganesha. Non-Hindus are not allowed admittance.

RECOMMENDATIONS

Bring insect repellent. Plan on a warm jacket since the evenings are cool.

Observation site

Senegal (Eastern Senegal): Niokolo Koba National Park

Some 380 species of birds populate the region, including red-throated bee-eaters.

The largest lions known are sheltered in a sparsely populated, densely vegetated area of southeastern Senegal—the Niokolo Koba, a national park created in 1954. The park extends for 4,878 sq mi (8,130 sq km) in the heart of a hot, dusty region that is one of the most beautiful in the country. Relatively passed over by mass tourism due to its distance from Dakar, the park is covered with a wooded savanna and light forests. Numerous plant species shelter the area's wildlife. This region is crossed by the Gambia, Niokolo Koba, and Koulountou rivers, which are bordered by thick forests.

The forests of Mount Assirik, 1,023 mi (310 m) high, shelter chimpanzee colonies. The place is the refuge of several dozen elephants as well as many other mammals and birds. At times in the grassy plains, leopards can be seen resting on acacia tree branches.

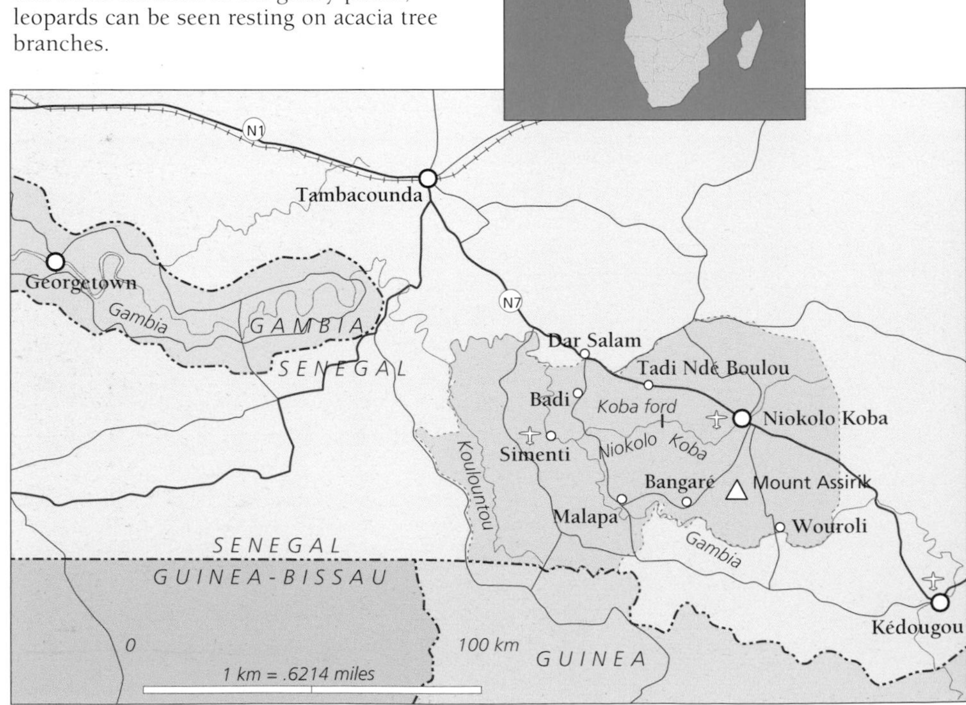

Warthogs, also called "wild pigs," are typically found in many areas of Africa.

Fauna and flora

The various ungulates of this region can be seen around watering holes: Derby elands, Buffon's kobs, Defassa waterbucks or crescent kobs, Roan antelope, water buffalo, ourebis, Grimm duikers, red-flanked duikers, warthogs, guibs harnaches, and buffalo. One can also observe hippopotami, rare giraffes (fewer than ten in 1978), red monkeys (or patas), populations of chimpanzees, Colobus monkeys, green monkeys, and baboons. Carnivores present are leopards, caracals, servals, various species of wild cats, civets, Villiers genets, tigrine genets, spotted hyenas, jackals, African

The Niokolo Koba park is covered with wooded savannas and light forests.

wild dogs, white-cheeked otters, and ichneumon mongooses as well as other species of mongoose. The rare aardvark, *orycteropus*, has also been observed. The region is also marked with large termite mounds. Also in this region are roughly 380 species of birds, among which we will only mention spatulas and ombrets. Species of crocodiles can also be found, as well as the Senegal chameleon, Nile varan, and some sixty species of fish including the strange protopterus and polypterus.

More than 1,500 plant species are represented, among which are bamboos (covering Mount Assirik), palms, and roniers.

Observation

The best time of year to visit Niokolo Koba is between February and May, since travel to the region is impractical during the rainy season (June and July), and dry fogs frequently mask the country during December and January. Morning and evening are the best times for observation.

In the dry season, the wildlife of the region is mainly visible around watering holes and permanent water courses such as the Cambia, Niokolo Koba, the buckle of Badi, Sitandi, Sibiloulou, Tourmadala, Mansafara, and Sanogolo ponds. The Simenti sector, to the west, is equally rich in wildlife. Some ten viewpoints facilitate observation. This region's lions are the largest known, and only one hundred or so remain. They are not always in sight and usually are seen when resting.

The park is open from November to June. You cannot move around the park during the night, nor on foot. Remember to drive slowly while negotiating the 360 mi (600 km) of trails that cut through the park (maximum speed is 15 mph; 25 km/h) to avoid hitting wandering animals and raising too much dust. All-terrain vehicles are necessary, and you should bring along food and water. Be sure to observe the animals from a good distance away so as not to disturb them.

Trips are organized from Dakar and Banjul (Gambia). You can also get to the park on your own, but you must be accompanied by an official guide within the park's limits. Three itineraries are particularly interesting: from Tadi Nde Boulou (N7) going toward the Koba ford, then traveling toward Simenti and toward Badi; from Niokolo Koba (N7) heading for the Wouroli ford and running along the Gambia River; and from Simenti leaving in the direction of the Bangare ford. It is possible to obtain information from, and make reservations with, the Office of National Parks, Point E, Dakar, BP 3135.

The lions of Niokolo Koba are the largest known; they are also often more cautious and difficult to observe. They spend the hot hours of the day sleeping in the shade of trees where they can find a bit of cool air and protect themselves from flies.

The lion in Africa

In Africa, the lion generally represents strength and power. As in certain European countries as well, it symbolizes nobility and royalty, which explains its presence on numerous emblems and flags.

Traditionally, the African tribal chief possessed a stick sculpted in the form of a lion to symbolize his power. Eating the lion's flesh and especially its heart was thought to confer great courage. According to certain African beliefs, chiefs were reincarnated as lions, or their souls inhabited the great cats' bodies.

Killing a lion by stabbing it through with a lance was one of the Masai rituals in which men attained the rank of warrior. According to the Masai, eating the lion's flesh or wearing parts of its body as ornaments allowed an individual to cure certain diseases and earn immortality.

The lion also was important in Egyptian civilization. The oldest portrait of the goddess Bastet, dating from 3,000 B.C., represents her with the head of a lioness. She symbolized the "blazing eye of the sun." Her sister, the goddess Sekhmet who was even more ferocious, was the symbol of war, the sun, and was also represented with a lioness' head. The tombs of the Egyptian pharaohs were decorated with sculpted lions; the lions were grouped in pairs, and placed back to back to signify their universality and their ambition to dominate all places and things. These same tombs were guarded by the Egyptian figure of the god-sun called the sphinx, a creature with a human head and the body of an outstretched lion. The most famous sphinx is located in Giza, near Cairo, a statue 128 ft (39 m) long and 56 ft (17 m) tall. The sphinx personified knowledge and its mysteries, and at the beginning represented the pharaohs. Later, it became the symbol of hidden knowledge and enigmas.

PRACTICAL INFORMATION

The best time to go to Niokolo Koba is between February and May.

TRANSPORTATION

■ **BY PLANE.** Paris is linked to Dakar by two daily flights (six hours). Flights depart from Dakar to Tambacounda, Simenti, Kedougou, or Niokolo Koba.

■ **BY CAR.** The road from Dakar to the Niokolo Koba park is good, approximately 366 mi (610 km). You'll need to take Route N1 to Tambacounda 283 mi (472 km), then take N7 toward Kedougou, until Dar Salam 50 mi (83 km); take the fork for the Simenti camp, located in the park, or continue straight to the Niokolo Koba camp 33 mi (55 km).

■ **BY TRAIN.** You can go by night train from Dakar to Tambacounda, then by bus or car to Simenti or Niokolo Koba.

CLIMATE

Temperatures: maximum from 88°–90° F (31°–32° C) (July–September) to 105° F (41° C) (April); minimum from 53° F (14°–15° C) (December–January) to 75°–77° F (24°–25° C) (May–June). Maximum monthly rainfall is in August, 11.4m (290 mm), with no rainfall from December to March. All year, there are seven to nine hours of sunlight a day.

LODGING

Several camps are on site, notably those of Niokolo Koba, the Lion, Malapa, and Bangare; the camp of Niokolo Koba is located on a magnificent site. One can also find hotels in Tambacounda, Simenti, and Badi.

VISITS

In the park's expanse to the east, N7 leads to Kedougou, principal city of Bassari country, where a bit further to the west Peuls and Boins can be found. However, the heart of the country is found 50 mi (80 km) from there, near Ebarakh at Etiolo. From Kedango, travel westward to Salemata, and from there, take the trail that runs northwest and leads to Etiolo. The Bassaris live in small individual huts 7 ft (2 m) in diameter, topped with conical straw roofs. The villages move several hundred meters approximately every two weeks. Numerous rituals are practiced and the young men and women undergo initiation rites that take place once every two years. Masked men come down from the hills shouting and playing whistles or cattle-bells. They bring the newly circumcised boys toward a "battlefield," keeping the women and children aside. After a confrontation, the ceremony continues through the night with dances and chants. The young initiates then leave for several nights in the brush to learn what a man must know about life, hunting, and the spirits.

RECOMMENDATIONS

It is imperative to inform the hotel of your itinerary before leaving. Never leave the trail, and return to the hotel before 6:30 P.M. Take extra water.

The Leopard

(Panthera pardus)

AFRIKAANS: luiperd — DUTCH: luipaard, panter
GERMAN: leopard, panther
FRENCH: panthére, léopard
SPANISH: leopardo — SWAHILI: chui

Description

The leopard, sometimes called the panther, has a supple body and broad head with short, rounded ears, a long tail, and large, powerful paws. The fur is dense and short-cropped, but rather long on individuals living in cold regions. The color of the back and sides varies from yellow or light tawny to orange-yellow, and from olive gray to gray-brown or olive brown. The underbelly is white to shades of gray or yellow. The head, nape of the neck, and belly are covered with black spots. The back and sides are decorated with rosettes made up of two to four black spots arranged in a circle. The coloration and the arrangement of the spots vary among individuals and by geographic origin. In some regions, leopards are darker, sometimes in shades of black on the back and sides or even totally black. These are called black leopards and were once thought to be a different species. These melanistic forms exist in the entire area of distribution, but are more frequent in certain regions. On the Malaysian peninsula, close to 50 percent of all leopards are melanistic. The young are darker with irregularly formed rosettes. The back of the ears are black, decorated with a white spot that becomes larger as the cat matures.

Measurements. Male: head and body length 52–76 in (130–190 cm); tail 28–40 in (70–100 cm); height at the withers 20–40 in (50–70 cm); weight 99–143 lb (45–65 kg). Female: head and body length 44–56 in (110–140 cm); tail 24–30 in (60–75 cm); height at the withers 18–24 in (45–60 cm); weight 77–110 lb (35–50 kg). Newborn: length 8 in (20 cm); tail 6 in (15 cm); weight 15 oz (430 g).

Lifespan. Generally leopards live up to 21 years in captivity, about 12 years in the wild.

Locomotion

The leopard is a tree-dweller, but hunts on the ground. It swims very well and can navigate moving water but not large rivers. The presence of water is not a necessity for leopards.

Activity

When not disturbed, the leopard is active during the day as well as at night. If it is disturbed, it becomes nocturnal, and is very cautious. It often lounges in the sun on a tree branch, its

Of the large cats, the leopard is probably best able to climb trees, in which it sometimes stores and safeguards its food.

arms and legs dangling, or on a rock. It begins to hunt most often at twilight.

Hunting and feeding

The leopard feeds on small and large mammals such as antelopes, gazelles, monkeys (especially baboons), kobs, zebras, lion cubs, young cheetahs, jackals, rodents, and many others, including those that weigh several times the leopard's weight. It also eats many birds, various reptiles, fish, insects, and domestic animals, such as sheep, goats, calves, and dogs. Its mid-range size is ideal because it allows the leopard to feed on a large variety of prey. Most often, its prey are ungulates that range from 44 to 110 lb (20 to 50 kg), but when this game becomes rare, the leopard attacks smaller animals such as monkeys, small carnivores, and the like. It also feeds on carrion. Generally, it drinks water every day, but can do without

The leopard is phenomenally strong. The leg and neck muscles are particularly powerful, as are those of the jaws, which enable the leopard to hoist prey into trees.

for several months because it gets sufficient fluid from its prey.

The leopard hunts alone, most often at night, on the ground rather than in trees. It finds its prey by sight rather than smell. It approaches the prey crouching, keeping behind cover, then springs upon the prey. After killing the animal, the leopard eviscerates it and carries it into a tree. It can store several carcasses in the same tree and reserved this way the carcasses last as much as four times longer than those left on the ground, since they are protected from scavengers and other predators.

Predators

Lions, African wild dogs, spotted hyenas, and crocodiles.

Social behavior

The leopard is solitary. The usual size of its territory varies from approximately 2.4 to 24 sq mi (60 sq km), but can be much greater—up to approximately 160 sq mi (400 sq km). The territory of a male includes the territory of one or several females. Generally, the females have separate hunting areas. Leopard territories vary according to environmental conditions and prey availability. Leopards defend their territories and mark them with sounds, urine spraying, and scratching the ground and trees. The vocal signal used to announce its presence and mark its hunting territory is a hoarse, low coughing sound repeated approximately ten times. When communicating by sound, leopards use certain signals for different kinds of contact. To signal approach it uses a hoarse grating sound, to indicate aggression it shrieks and roars, to show satisfaction it purrs. The female greets its young with a quiet "peep peep peep."

Reproduction

Leopards give birth in the spring in subtropical regions, and all year round in tropical regions. The female comes into estrus roughly every 45 days for 6 to 7 days; during estrus she is courted by several males. Gestation generally lasts from 90 to 112 days, then the female gives birth in a sheltered spot like a burrow, hollow tree, or clump of bushes. Litters range from one to six young (most often two or three). Cubs open their eyes at 1 week; nursing lasts 3 months. At that age, they begin to accompany their mother when she roams and they learn to hunt. The cubs leave her when they are around 12 to 18 months old and mature sexually between 2½ and 3 years of age.

Distribution

The leopard has the widest distribution of any cat and is adapted to the greatest variety of habitats. It is found in the most arid regions as well as the dampest habitats. Leopards need hiding places to lie in wait, and can use the slightest irregularity of terrain, or even small tufts of grass, to approach their prey without being seen. They easily adapt, and can be found even in the suburbs of Nairobi and other large African cities. The leopard can be found throughout Africa and in Zanzibar, but has practically disappeared north of the 20th parallel North (although it may survive in Algeria and Morocco), as well as from a good portion of South Africa, Uganda, and Somalia. Outside Africa, it is found in Oman, Saudi Arabia, and the United Arab Emirates, and in Yemen, Israel, Afghanistan,

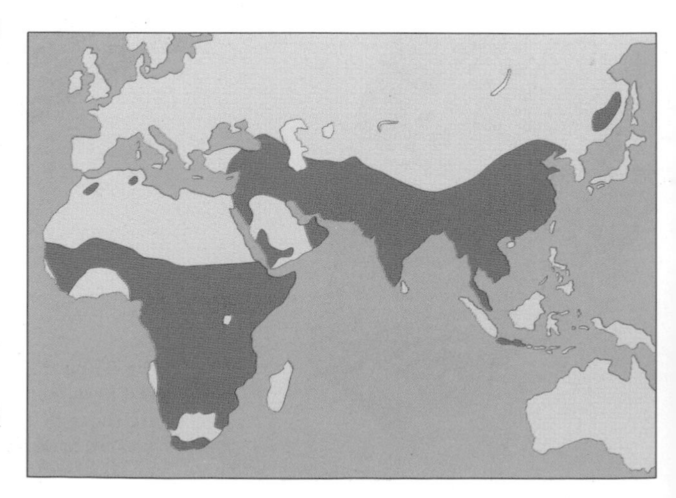

Armenia, Azerbaijan, Georgia, Iran, Tadjikistan, Turkey, Turkmenistan, and Uzbekistan. It is also found in India, Sri Lanka, Indonesia, Korea, China, and Russia.

Status

Leopards are extremely endangered in a large portion of their range. The market for leopard fur coats is largely responsible for their decline, but leopards were also hunted for attacking cattle, and for this reason are not popular with cattle ranchers.

Historical overview

The species *Panthera pardus* is generally called the leopard in Africa and the panther in Asia. In many countries the leopard symbolizes strength. In China, it was said that the leopard announced the change of seasons. In Egypt, it was associated with Seth, the god of evil. During funeral ceremonies the priests wore a leopard skin. In Benin, the leopard represented royal authority. In many areas of Africa, it is considered a totem. Several legends of leopard-men exist, and these are also found in India.

During the neolithic period in Anatolia, a leopard cult existed that was associated with the goddess of fertility. In the West, the leopard symbolizes the virtues of the warrior.

Researchers have advanced one theory concerning human evolution and our relationship to the leopard. Based on observations of carcasses left by leopards in trees, researchers think the first hominids may have used these carcasses as an easily accessible food source. This behavior has been observed in baboons.

The leopard uses its keen eyesight to locate its prey. It sneaks up on its prey, approaching the animal as closely as possible before jumping onto its back, seizing it by the throat and choking it.

Observation site

Indonesia (Java): Ujung Kulon

On the island of Java in Indonesia, over two-thirds of the primal forest has remained untouched; it's a dense jungle that's difficult to traverse and it makes a good hiding place for rare animals, including the few remaining Javan rhinoceroses. The tiger has disappeared from the island, but the leopard remains. It's possible to see the last Indonesian leopards in the western portion of Java, on the Ujung Kulon peninsula that advances into the strait of the Sonde, a short distance from the famous Krakatoa volcano.

The Ujung Kulon preserve that includes the peninsula and the island of Panaitan is protected on one side by the sea and on the other by mountains. This explains why it has been possible to preserve the natural environment there. In addition, this area is one of the last Javanese bastions of the rain forest's original flora. All of the wildlife native to Java can be found in this preserve, but you'll have to cross the jungle and the thick forests bordering the rivers to get there.

Fauna and flora

The jungle of this Indonesian island shelters numerous monkeys, such as silvery gibbons, leaf monkeys of the Sonde islands, ebony leaf monkeys, macaques, and slow lorises. You can also find wild boars as well as deer such as the muntjac, sambar deer, rusa deer of Timor, and bovines such as bantengs. Among the other mammals, you can find flying squirrels, porcupines, civets, palm

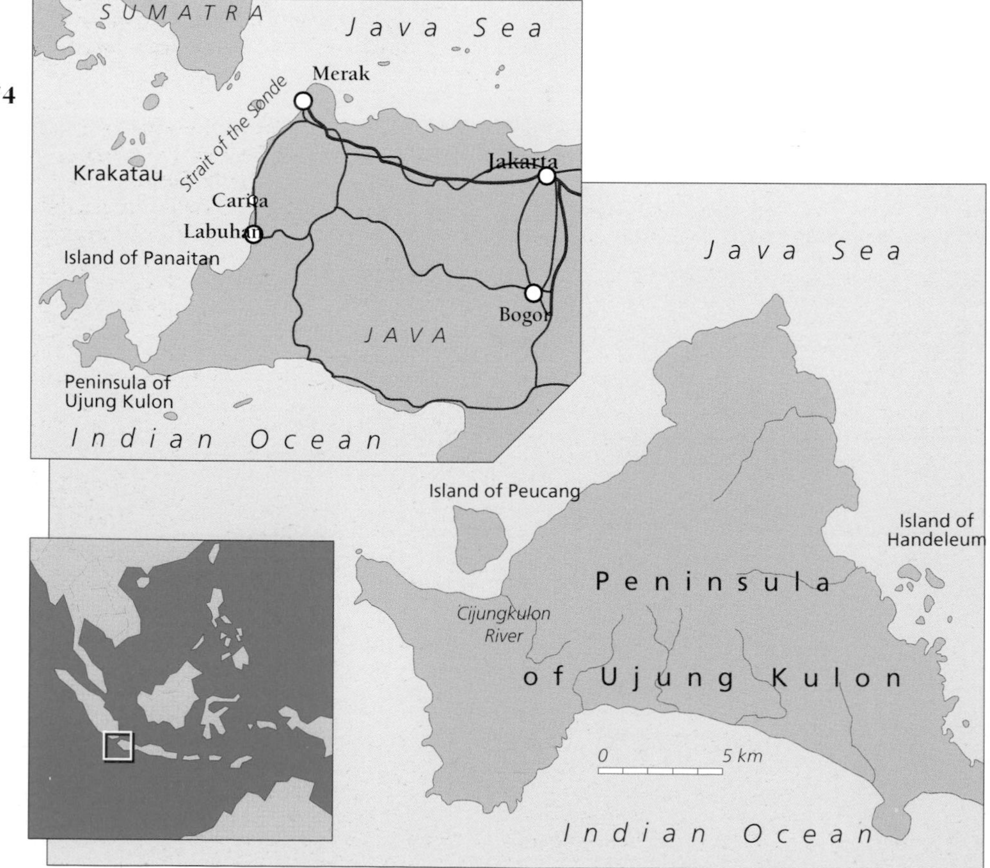

civets, and binturongs. Numerous birds including calaos and peacocks populate the forest, as well as reptiles such as crocodiles, iguanas, and many snakes. The island of Java is covered with a dense and varied vegetation including heveas, teas, pandanus, and coconut palms, and forests of teak, mahogany, and sandalwood.

The eruption of the Krakatoa volcano in 1883 destroyed most of the island on which it was located. In 1927, a new eruption created the Anak Krakatoa.

Observation

The best time to visit the Ujung Kulon preserve is from May to October in order to avoid the rainy season. Leopards are best observed at dawn. It's difficult to get to this region and it's necessary to prepare your trip well in advance. You must plan several days of travel to reach the preserve, in addition to the observation trip itself. Ujong Kulon can be explored on foot or by boat, and you can choose to be accompanied by a guide or not, it's up to you. However, a forest guide is indispensable because the wildlife, hiding in the dense jungle, is difficult to see.

The leopards are among the most secretive animals of Java. To catch a glimpse of one of

The Wallace line

Naturalist Alfred Wallace (1823-1913) was one of the pioneers of biogeography and contributed to further studies of the theory of evolution. In 1856, he discovered that in Bali the bird species (the same as those on the island of Java), were not found on the nearby island of Lombok. He traced what came to be called the "Wallace line," which passes between Bali and Lombok and between Borneo and the Celebes. This line clearly marks biogeographic zones. To the west live tigers, various monkeys including orangutans, bears, and so on. The east is populated by birds of paradise and marsupials such as cuckoos and tree kangaroos. Therefore, the islands of Bali and Lombok, so close in size and climate and having identical topography, each have totally different wildlife.

The first explanation for this discovery was that the sea between these two islands is very deep. Bali is located on the continental plateau and was formerly joined to Java and the other islands, whereas Lombok is situated in a zone of deep sea. However, it wasn't until Wegener (1880-1930) put forth his continental drift theory that it was understood that until very recently Bali and Lombok were not adjacent, which perfectly explained the wildlife differences.

On the other hand, the colonization of the islands remains a mystery. For a long time it was thought that the oceans formed impassable barriers, but in reality, many islands were populated even though no longer linked to the continent. The theory explaining this claims that natural rafts detached from the coast, taking flora and fauna across the oceans. These natural Noah's arks could have been aided by a proximity no longer existent today due to continental drift.

Besides the macaques (above), silvery gibbons, leaf monkeys, and slow lorises live in Java.

leopards rest. Leopards can also be seen walking on the banks. Don't overlook a trip to the Cijungkulon river, where herds of bantengs graze.

To enter the park, you must have a visitor's permit that can be obtained at the nature protection service (PHPA) of Bogor (J1. Juanda 9, bogor; open mornings). Bungalow reservations are necessary. Brochures on the park are available at the general office of tourism in Jakarta (9 jln Merdeka Selatan, Jakarta). Your excursion must be well planned; you must arrange food and lodging from Labuhan, and you must be in good physical condition. You can rent a boat to reach the peninsula or join a group from Carita. If you choose to be accompanied by a guide, the guide will obtain the necessary authorizations.

these magnificent animals you must be lucky, observe tracks well, and be equipped with a good pair of binoculars. Your best bet is to leave on an observation trip at dawn, and inspect the trees bordering the rivers where

PRACTICAL INFORMATION

The best time to visit Ujung Kulon is May to October.

TRANSPORTATION

■ **BY PLANE.** The flight from Paris to Jakarta takes 18 hours.
■ **BY CAR.** From Jakarta, take the highway leading to Merak toward the west, then go south to Labuhan or all the way to Carita. The distance from Jakarta to Labuhan is 90 mi (figure on four hours by car approximately). Once there, you can access the preserve by boat, (4 to 5 hours) either on government vedette-boats, or on fishing boats. By car, the road is very difficult and you need to allow 2 days.
■ **BY BUS OR TRAIN.** You can also get from Jakarta to Merak by train or bus, and to Labuhan by bus or taxi.

CLIMATE

The temperature fluctuates between 76°–78° F (23°–24° C) and 84°–86° F (29°–30° C) throughout the year. Rainfall in western Java reaches 12 in (300 mm) per month in January and February, and it drops to less than 2 in (45 mm) per month in August. During the rainy season, the water falls in waterspouts; the rains are spaced from mid-May to mid-November and fall no more than once a day in the afternoon, which allows you to take walks. Sunshine ranges from four to eight hours a day.

LODGING

You can camp in the forest or stay in the bungalows on the island of Peucang or Handeleum. Food must be arranged for the entire length of the stay.

VISITS

The volcanic island of Krakatoa in the middle of the strait of the Sonde is approximately 24 mi (40 km) northeast of Labuhan. You can get there from Labuhan by renting a boat or taking an organized tour. Many beautiful archeological sites also can be visited in Java, such as the Buddhist temple of Borobudur situated 25 mi northwest of Jogyakarta, and the Hindu site of Prahbanan (10 mi northeast of Jogyakarta).

RECOMMENDATIONS

Plan your trip carefully and arrange for everything needed well in advance, including food and drink, because the park is located in the jungle.

Observation site

Zimbabwe: Hwange National Park

It seems as if all the beauty of Africa is gathered in Zimbabwe. Its green valleys between its rocky heights have earned it the name "the Switzerland of Africa." One remarkable feature of this country is the legendary Victoria Falls. One thousand twenty miles high, the falls plunge into the gorges of the Zambeze, forming clouds of water droplets visible at a distance of 24 mi (40 km) in all directions. Downstream lies lake Kariba, one of the largest artificial lakes in the world. This lake has engulfed miles of forest and has become an extraordinary gathering place for elephants, hippos, and birds. To the southwest are the hills of Matopo. These eroded rocks of granite have caves with superb rupestral paintings that are several thousands of years old. To the east rise mountains. Everywhere extraordinary wildlife can be found, and the list of animal species there would number in the thousands.

The portrait of Zimbabwe would be incomplete if one did not mention the astonishing archeological site that gave the country its name, the ancient city called "Great Zimbabwe" founded in the year 1200.

The national park of Hwange (formerly Wankie), is situated in the west and extends for 8,400 mi (14,000 km). Several hundred leopards live in this region.

Fauna and flora

In addition to the leopards you can find in Hwange Park, you can observe herds of elephants numbering up to 100, several hundred lions, cheetahs, wild dogs, jackals, genets, civets, various mongooses, spotted hyenas, buffaloes, wildebeest, kudus, hartebeest, impalas, zebras, rhinoceroses, aardvarks, panjolins, baboons, vervets, as well as approximately 400 species of birds, including pink flamingos, scissorbeaks, pelicans, coursers and pratincoles, bulbuls, jacanas, circaetus,

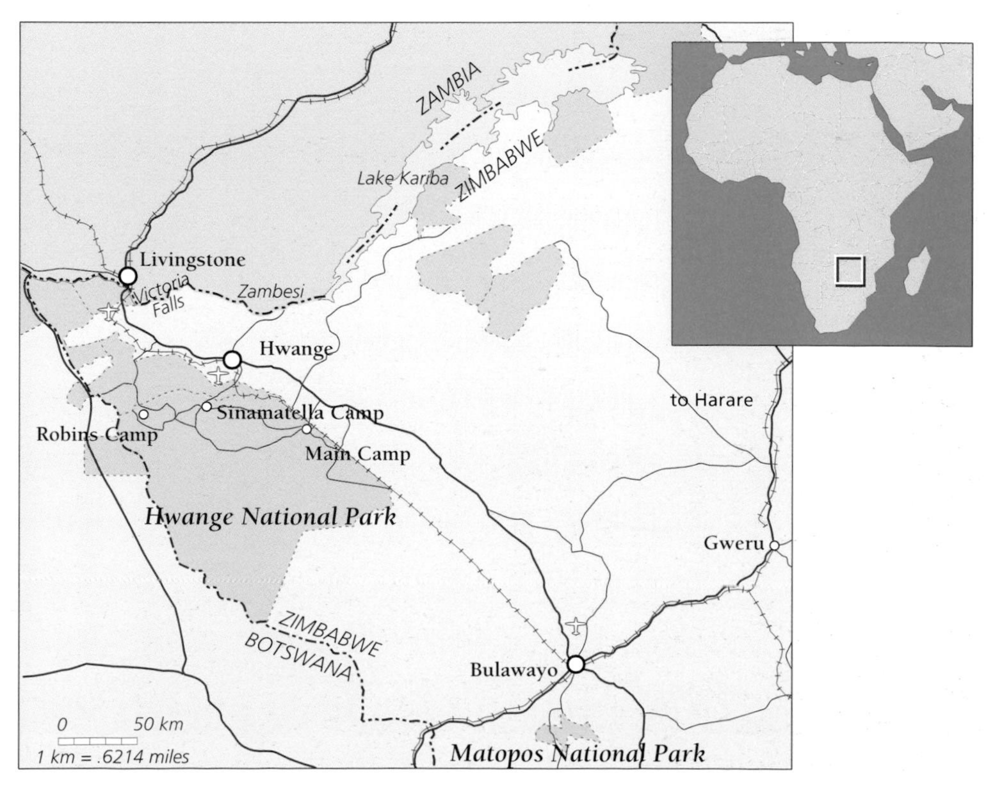

The intense heat leads to the use of readily available insulating materials, such as earth and plants, for traditional housing.

calaos, ostriches, and outards. Zimbabwe is known to have the most sightings of royal leopards, whose spots join to form black stripes.

The vegetation is composed essentially of mopane and baobabs.

Observation

The best time to go to Zimbabwe is April to October. At the Hwange National Park, ponds provide the best wildlife viewing, the busiest of those being Nyamandhlovet Guvalala (near the Main Camp), which is particularly rich in minerals. You will see

Hwange Park's vegetation is composed of thorn bushes, mopane, and baobabs.

ungulates in particular, but other animals go there as well. Leopards are not the easiest felines to see in Africa because of their habit of dwelling in trees. Patience and a good pair of binoculars are required to spot them. They are active particularly at night; by day, they rest in the trees and can be seen at dawn and twilight. Nighttime expeditions are possible by the light of the full moon, which allows you to see leopards during their period of activity; obviously, this is ideal. The Hwange Park includes a network of 289 mi (482 km) of roads, on which you can travel by renting a four-wheel-drive vehicle. You can also get there by joining an organized safari with a guide. As in any other place, it's important to move slowly and not approach the animals too closely.

Livingston

Beginning in 1841, Protestant missionary and explorer, David Livingston (1813–1873), took a series of trips to central and southern Africa. First guided by humanitarian concern since he opposed slavery, he later sought to discover trade routes for the Europeans, a practical goal to complement his altruistic aims.

During one of his principal voyages, he left from Linyanti, at the center of southern Africa, and continued northwest to Luanda on the Atlantic coast. He then retraced his steps and traveled eastward. This trip took him the length of the Zambeze river, where in 1855 he saw the steam from what the Makololos call "the smoke which growls"—the falls of the Zambeze that he named Victoria Falls as a tribute to Queen Victoria. These falls are situated 900 mi (1500 km) from the source of the Zambeze. He continued his route to Quelimane on the East coast, completing the first crossing of Africa from west to east. He then tried to open a commercial route on the Zambeze, but his attempts failed due to the enormous rapids that lowered the depth of the river.

His explorations made him famous when he returned to England. With the death of Speke in 1864, he was asked to continue the former's research on the sources of the Nile. Therefore, in 1966 he began a long trip, during which he lost all contact with the rest of the world, but used the opportunity to investigate the slave trade. It was Stanley, an American journalist, who found him one day and greeted him with those now famous words: "Doctor Livingston, I presume?"

With the new equipment Stanley brought, Livingston departed again in search of the sources of the Nile, but before attaining his goal he became very ill and died in 1873 at Ilala, near lake Bangweulu. Stanley completed Livingston's work and confirmed Speke's discovery, proving that Lake Victoria was truly the beginning of the Nile.

PRACTICAL INFORMATION

The best time to go to Zimbabwe is from April to October.

TRANSPORTATION

■ **BY PLANE.** Flights link Paris to Harare. Domestic flights to Victoria Falls, Bulawayo or Kariba also exist. From Bulawayo, an air link leads to Hwange.

■ **BY CAR.** From Harare, you can travel by road to Hwange, either passing through the region of Lake Kariba, or via Bulawayo. The distance from Harare to Hwange is 463 mi (771 km). The park is accessible by three entrances: Main Camp, Sinamatella Camp, and Robins Camp.

■ **BY TRAIN.** Trains link Harare and Hwange.

CLIMATE

Temperatures: maximum from 81° F (27° C) (June-July) to 98°–100° F (36°–37° C) (October-November); minimum from 52° F (11° C) (June-July) to 72° F (22° C) (October-November). The rainy season lasts from November to March, with maximum rain in January and February (6 in/month). From April to October, precipitation is light 0 to .7 in/month (0 to 18 mm/month). There are six to ten hours of sun a day.

LODGING

To stay in the parks, advance reservations are required and can be booked by contacting: Central Booking Office, P.O. Box CY 140, Causeway or Bulawayo Booking Agency, P.O. Box 2283, Bulawayo. It is also possible to camp or to rent bungalows in the park at Main Camp, Sinamatella Camp, and Robins Camp.

VISITS

Victoria Falls are an exceptional point of interest. They are accessible by plane, train, or road. You can fly over them in a light plane. Downstream, Lake Kariba is a good destination. You can rent a boat and observe hippos, crocodiles, and elephants.

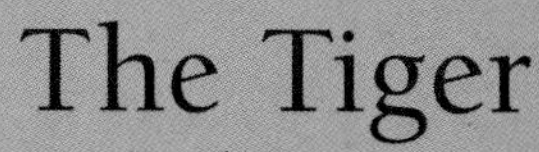

The Tiger

(Panthera tigris)
DUTCH: tijger — FRENCH: Le tigre
GERMAN: tiger
IN INDIA AND NEPAL: bagh — SPANISH: tigre

Description

The tiger is the largest feline. Its face is short and its ears small and rounded. Its hind legs are longer than the front, an adaptation that aids jumping. It is a powerfully muscled animal.

The tiger is the only large striped feline; the stripes are good camouflage for a forest habitat. They are black and form intersecting bands over the entire body. The undercoat on the back and sides vary from orange to reddish; the underbelly, tip of the muzzle, and the area around the eyes are creamy white. The back of the ears is black with a white spot. The tail is long and striped. A ruff frames the head. The color of the fur, the design of the stripes, and the length of the hairs vary according to geographical origin.

Measurements. Head and body length 56–112 in (140–280 cm); tail 24–36 in (60–95 cm); weight: male 440–594 lb (200–270 kg); female 275–352 lb (125–160 kg). Newborn: 44–72 oz (1100–1800 g). The Siberian tiger is the largest of the species and can weigh up to 845 lb. (384 kg).

Lifespan. Tigers live approximately 15 years in the wild and up to 20 years in captivity.

Locomotion

Tigers are good runners, even if they do not pursue their prey for long. Above all, they are excellent swimmers and can cross rivers. Tigers must have water to survive.

Activity

Tigers hunt between twilight and dawn. They usually sleep during the day, but occasionally nursing females hunt in the daytime.

Hunting and feeding

Tigers feed on all the large prey they can catch: deer, wild pigs, gaurs, and buffalo, but also on hares, lynx, and badgers (the last three live in Siberia). They also catch fish and crustaceans. The diet varies according to the animal's region. Tigers will kill cattle and attack humans rather frequently. They are good runners, but hunt by stalking. The tiger covers great distances in search of prey. When prey is spotted, the tiger tracks it and stays under cover as long as possible, camouflaged in the vegetation because of its striped fur. When the tiger comes within 11–22 yd (10–20 m) of its prey, it pounces. Most often, the attack comes from behind.

The tiger knocks down the prey and kills it either by biting the back of the neck, crushing the neck vertebrae, or by seizing the throat in a suffocating hold. It drags the prey to a sheltered area and begins to feed, usually first upon the hindquarters. The tiger then eviscerates the animal and continues to feed. Tigers can eat large quantities of meat in a single meal, and small animals are devoured at once. Large prey serves as food for several days. The tiger alternates between eating and sleeping until the food is gone. A tiger requires 20 lb (9 kg) of meat per day. It drinks often and cannot do without water.

Predators

None, except humans. The young can sometimes be killed by hyenas or large dog species such as wolves or dholes.

Social behavior

Tigers are solitary, but apparently tolerate one another quite well. In fact, one can find groups, generally made up of females and their young, but occasionally composed of a male and female. In captivity, tigers sometimes maintain groups, which shows a high degree of social tolerance. However, in nature, they live in a relatively closed environment with scattered

Gestation lasts approximately 194 to 106 days; the female alone raises her young, which she nurses for about six months. The cubs consume their first meal of meat around 2 or 3 months, and hunt by themselves at around 18 months of age.

prey, and therefore solitary hunting is more productive than cooperation. The size of a tiger's territory varies from 6–400 sq mi (16–1,000 sq km), depending on the amount of available prey. The females' territories may overlap, particularly when raising young. For males, territories are larger and cover the territory of several females. Tigers mark their territory with feces and urine and by scratching tree trunks. These marks, which are renewed regularly, indicate the tiger's presence and help avoid confrontations, but occasional conflicts occur nevertheless.

Reproduction

A male's territory includes that of several females with whom he can mate. He eliminates possible competition for food by preventing other tigers from entering the territory. Mating takes place in any season, especially in tropical zones, but most often from November to April. In the most Nordic regions, the reproductive period is limited to winter. The female is sexually receptive for several days, and mating can take place up to 100 times in 2 days. Generally, gestation lasts 104 to 106 days, and the litters are usually composed of two or three young. The female raises her young alone. Cubs open their eyes between 1 and 17 days of age. They nurse for six months and begin to eat solid food after about 2 or 3 months. At that time the mother brings her young to the carcasses of her prey. At 1 year, young tigers become more independent but are still not completely capable of hunting alone. Around 18 months, they kill game themselves but continue to use their mother's territory. Usually, they become truly independent between 18 and 30 months. They reach sexual maturity around the age of 3 to 4 years.

Distribution

Tigers are found in varied habitats and climates, as long as sufficient plant cover and year round water are present. They are found in the taiga, tropical or dry forests, and in mangrove swamps. Tigers exist in Bangladesh, Bhutan, Cambodia, China, India, Indonesia (in Sumatra), Laos, Malaysia, Burma, Nepal, Russia, Thailand, and Vietnam. They have been found in North Korea, but are possibly extinct in that area now.

Status

The tiger is an endangered species, with probably no more than 2,500 adult animals in the wild. Three subspecies (the tigers of the Caspian Sea, Bali, and Java) have been extinct since the 1950s.

Historical overview

Researchers believe that at the beginning of this century between 40,000 and 50,000 tigers existed in India alone. Their numbers fell in that country to less than 2,000 by the end of the 1960s. The destruction of their habitat and human population growth alone cannot explain this sharp drop in numbers. No, hunting is to blame. In fact, for more than two centuries, the maharajahs and English governors enjoyed the sport of tiger hunting that turned into pure and simple massacres. Indeed, one such "sportsman" would brag of having killed 616 tigers in his lifetime, another 170 in 36 years; the deaths of up to

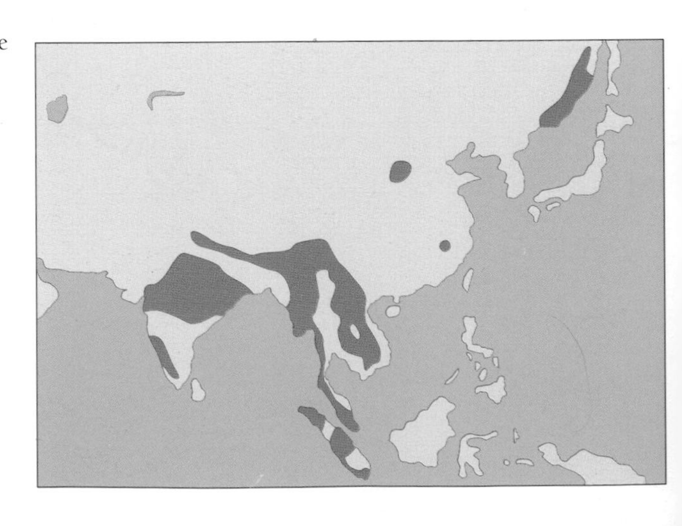

1,000 tigers have been attributed to Colonel Kesari Singh, the head of the Department of the Hunt of the states of Gwalior and Jaipur, and 800 have been attributed to Maharajah Madho Rao de Gwalior. English lords also flaunted their hunting skills. Moreover, local populations trapped tigers to defend their herds or to sell the furs.

In 1969, the International Union for the Preservation of Nature (IUPN) alerted the public to the slaughter. In 1972, Indira Gandhi, then Prime Minister of India, with the help of the World Wildlife Fund (WWF) and the Smithsonian Institute in Washington, established the Tiger Project. From that point, tiger hunting in India was totally prohibited. The Corbett and Dudhawa National Parks were the first to protect the tiger, followed at first by nine, then by 15 other preserves.

In China, tigers are killed for their bones, which are used in Chinese medicine. Everywhere tigers are found, they are poached by cattle owners and hunted for their fur. In Russia, their numbers were estimated at between 150 and 200 in 1994; in the mid-1980s, there had been 250 to 430. Even now, protection measures ought to be able to stop this decline. The Russian tigers belong to the subspecies *altaica*. It's thought that no more than 250 specimens can remain now, if they still survive at all in China and in North Korea. The subspecies of southern China is thought to have dwindled to fewer than 50 individuals. In Sumatra, there cannot be more than 250 adults remaining.

The vast distribution of the tiger, encompassing both tropical and cold regions, can make it seem that the tiger is an animal who can adapt to all environments. Not so. In fact, the tiger is highly specialized and requires very specific ecological conditions. The tiger used to be found in all of Asia; then its distribution was sharply reduced as its need for large prey and forest areas became ever more difficult to satisfy.

Finally, tiger attacks in India result in a certain number of tiger deaths. When a tiger kills a human for the first time, the danger is that he will kill again since humans are easy prey, and the tiger will become a "man-eater." Sometimes, tigers turn to hunting humans when they are wounded and can no longer hunt their customary prey. To avoid this from happening, Indian authorities have put a plan into practice: in zones frequented by tigers, guards set up dummies dressed as villagers and permeated with human scent, but that deliver an electric shock when attacked. Hopefully, this system will dissuade tigers from attacking humans.

The tiger is a symbol in Asia, but it was also a choice hunting trophy. Today the tiger is totally protected, but several subspecies are already extinct, and the others are extremely endangered.

Observation site

India (Madhya Pradesh): Kanha and Bandhavgarh

The region of Madhya Pradesh is situated in the center of India. It occupies a vast plateau with a very hot climate. The district has a rich history, and has an abundance of fortified cities, palaces, and extraordinary temples. The province is equally remarkable for its forests, which shelter a rich fauna. The creation of preserves protects and perpetuates the wild animals of the jungle. The preserves offer a privileged meeting place for humans and animals.

The Kanha Preserve, 175 southeast of Jabalpur, is a beautiful area of forests and pasture lands irrigated by rivers. This preserve was the setting for the adventures of Mowgli in the *Jungle Book* by Rudyard Kipling, who was charmed by the region's beauty and abundant wildlife. It was created in 1955 to protect the swamp deer *Cervus duvauceli branderi*, also called barasingha, which hides under the teaks and bamboos of the Banjar valley forest to the west, and the Hallon valley forest to the east. You can also find Kipling's "Sher Khan," and indeed, the reserve is part of the Tiger Project.

A bit farther north, the Bandhavgarh Park shelters a greater concentration of tigers than are present at Kanha. It is located 118 mi

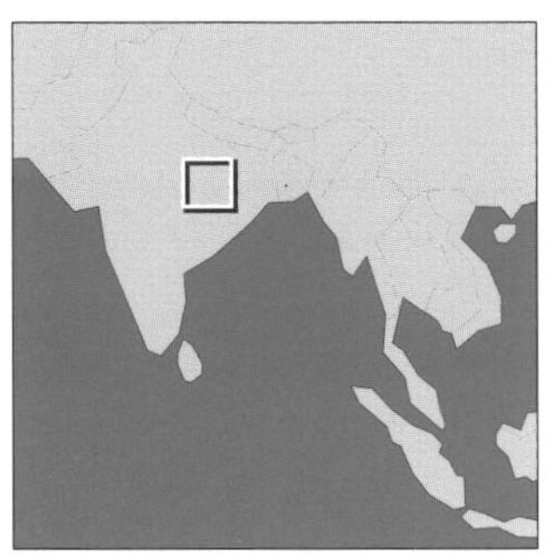

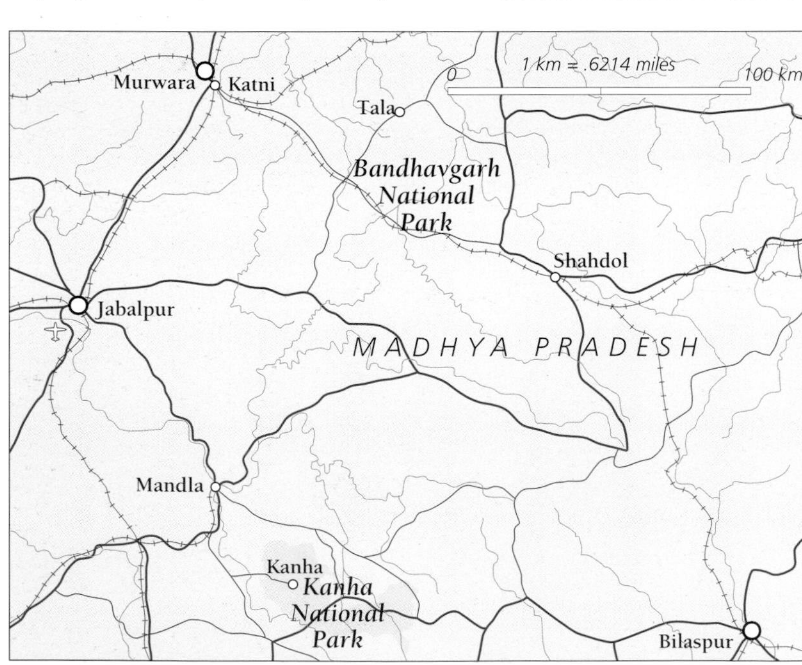

(197 km) northeast of Jabalpur, in the Vindhyan mountains, a spot dominated by a cliff on which a temple sits, surrounded by a fortress. In the forests of the Madhya Pradesh region also lives the famous "Baloo," the sloth bear with its ruffled fur and powerful claws. These regions are covered with dense jungle and must be crossed on the back of an elephant or in an all-terrain vehicle if you are to be initiated into the Law of the Jungle.

Fauna and flora

This preserve shelters the barasingha, as well as black deer, chitals, Indian buffalo, gaurs (Indian cows), nilgai, warthogs, langur monkeys, porcupines, leopards, hyenas, sloth bears, civets and mongooses, canines called dholes *(Cuon alpinus)* or Asian wild dogs, and, among the many species of birds, black ibises. Many snakes, including pythons and cobras, can also be found. The forest consists of teaks and bamboo.

In India, tiger attacks are not uncommon. Humans try to protect themselves with masks placed on the back of the head to trick the tiger into thinking it can't sneak up on them from behind.

The forests of Madhya Pradesh shelter a rich fauna of ungulates (here, *Cervus duvauceli*), potential prey for the tiger.

Transport on the backs of elephants is the safest way to visit the parks of Madhya Pradesh.

Rudyard Kipling

Born in 1865 in Bombay, India, Rudyard Kipling was sent in 1871 to England where his mother later met him. In 1882, after his studies, he returned to India and worked as a journalist in Lahore. He wrote poems and novels inspired by India, which were published in 1887. In 1889, he returned to England and set up residence in London. He traveled to Japan, New Zealand, and Australia. In 1892, he married an American woman and departed to live in Vermont. It was there that he wrote the two volumes of the *Jungle Book* as well as *Captains Courageous*, published in England upon his return in 1896. He received the Nobel Prize for Literature in 1907 and died in London in 1936.

The *Jungle Book* is a collection of stories that take place in the Indian jungle. Wolves adopt a lost child, whom they call Mowgli, which means "frog." Rudyard Kipling describes life in the Indian jungle and its inhabitants: the black leopard Bagheera, the bear Baloo, the python Kaa, the tiger Sher Khan and many others. Life is controlled by the Law of the Jungle. A quick view can be seen in this excerpt from the first volume of the *Jungle Book*.

The Law of the Jungle, which orders nothing without a reason, forbids all beasts to eat man, except when it kills to show its children how to kill, in which case it must hunt outside of the preserves of its clan or its tribe. The real reason for this is that killing a man means, sooner or later, the invasion of white men armed with rifles and riding on elephants, and of brown men, by the hundreds, equipped with gongs, rockets, and torches. Then everyone suffers in the jungle.... The rationale that the animals give one another is that man, being the weakest and the most disarmed of living things, is unworthy of a hunter's touch. They say also, and it is true, that the eaters of men become mangy and lose their teeth. (*sic*)

Rudyard Kipling, *The Jungle Book*

Observation

The best time to go to Madhya Pradesh is between February and May. In March and April, when it is hot, the tigers leave the forest to travel to watering holes. Wildlife must be observed from the back of an elephant or in a jeep, with the mandatory guide present. Visitors are driven to areas where tigers are sighted in advance (*tiger shows*). The animals are obviously wild, even if it seems that some of them have become accustomed to the presence of humans, which simplifies approaching them.

Your chances of seeing tigers are best in the morning, since tigers are rarely active during the day. The jungle wildlife is wary and shy, and constant vigilance is needed to spot the animals. A pair of binoculars and a patient, competent guide are indispensable. For safety reasons, traffic in the park at night is prohibited.

PRACTICAL INFORMATION

The best time to go to Madhya Pradesh is between February and May.

TRANSPORTATION

■ **BY PLANE.** Regular flights run between Paris and Bombay. In Bombay, take a flight for Jabalpur.

■ **BY CAR, TRAIN, AND BUS.** From Jabalpur, you can reach Kanha by car or state bus (two a day for Kisli Gate, the entrance to Kanha). On site, you can rent a jeep. To reach Bandhavgarh, take the railroad or the road from Jabalpur to Katni. The park is found on the way in the direction of Bilaspur. Umaria is the nearest station at 19 mi (32 km). Buses link Umaria to Tala to reach Bandhavgarh.

CLIMATE

Temperatures: maximum from 82°–84° F (28°–29° C) (December to January) to 104°–109° F (40°–43° C) (April to May); minimum of 58° F (14° C) (December and January) to 78°–82° F (26°–28° C) (May and June). The rains are heavy from June to September, 7 to 16 in/month (175 to 405 mm/month); they are light (less than 1 in per month, .1 to .8 in (3 to 22 mm/month) from November to May. The sunniest period is between November and May (nine to ten hours a day) and the least sun is in July and August (three to four hours).

LODGING

Hotels can be found on the Jabalpur road and near Kisli Gate in Kanha. Make reservations through the State offices of tourism in Bombay, or the office of tourism in the Jabalpur station. Hotels and restaurants are located at the entrance to the park of Bandhavgarh in the village of Tala.

VISITS

In 1951, a white tiger cub was found near Bandhavgarh. It was named Mohun. He was mated with one of his daughters in 1958 and a litter of white tigers was born. Mohun's descendants are scattered in zoos throughout the world. They are not albinos; their eyes are blue and the stripes are present. This unusual coat is due to a recessive gene. When he died, Mohun's body was preserved and now is kept at the palace of the Maharajah of Rewa in Tala. Specimens of white tigers can be seen in zoos in India (New Delhi, Calcutta, Bhubanesvar, Mysore, Kanpur, Hyderabad, and Assam), and in several American and English zoos.

RECOMMENDATIONS

Heed the safety guidelines and do not venture anywhere alone.

White tigers have been artificially bred and are scattered in zoos worldwide. They are not albinos — note the presence of stripes. True albinos are extremely rare.

Observation site

Nepal (Terai): Royal Park of Bardia

The Terai is a fertile province of Nepal, famous for its protected flora and fauna. It extends over the entire northern part of the large plain of the Ganges, the zone that straddles northern India and southern Nepal. This area's subtropical climate is very different from one's usual image of Nepal: high mountain peaks and treks through snow.

The royal park of Bardia, situated to the west of the Terai, is one of the largest wildernesses of Nepal. It extends over 387 sq mi (968 sq km). Confined to the north by the hills of Churias, the park is bordered on the west by the Geruwa river, a small branch of the Karnali, which is one of the largest tributaries of the Ganges. The Karnali emerges at Chisapani. This park is covered with sal forests, prairies, savannas, and dense forests the length of the rivers. In this region of Nepal, you have the greatest chance of seeing a tiger. The region has areas of low vegetation favorable for spotting animals. One-horned rhinoceroses from the park of Chitwan (situated southwest of Katmandou) were introduced in 1986. A few wild elephants remain; the elephants in Nepal's other parks are domesticated.

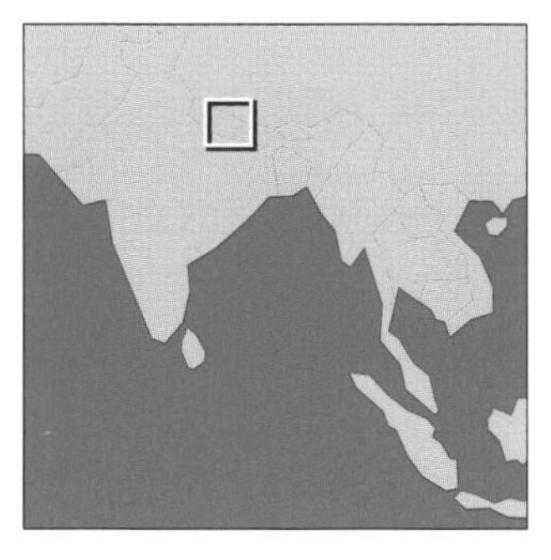

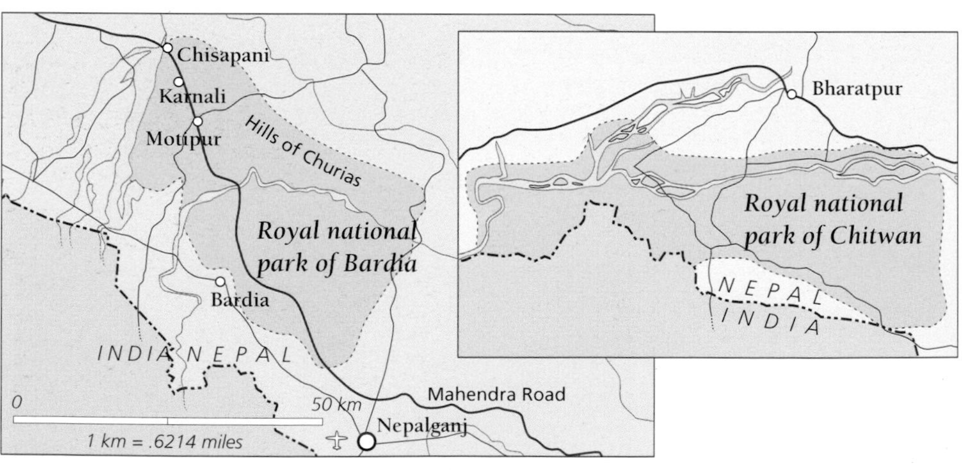

Fauna and flora

A great variety of monkeys are found in this region: entels, brown-red monkeys, and rhesus macaques; but also elephants, rhinoceroses, chitals, muntjacs, sambars, deer-pigs, swamp deer, Bengal deer, nilgais, and porcupines. The carnivores present are tigers, leopards, jungle cats, jackals, civets, palm civets, mongooses, sloth bears, and Asian black bears. The Geruwa river that flows out at Chisapani shelters mahseer fish, gavials, swamp crocodiles, as well as one of the rare fresh water cetaceans, the Ganges dolphin.

This region boasts 250 species of birds. You can observe cormorants, egrets,

The Terai's flora is rich and often brightly colored like this flamboyant tree.

Rhinos had disappeared from Bardia. All rhinos in the park of Chitwan have been reintroduced.

herons, storks, different species of ducks and geese, gobe-mouches, calaos, parrots, as well as the Bengal florican and the superb antigone crane.

The flora of the Terai consists of sal, a precious wood, as well as kapok trees, shishanis, and simals with large red flowers.

Observation

The best time to go to the park of Bardia is between September and May. The prime viewing time is the morning or at twilight.

You can observe tigers safely from the back of an elephant; when a tiger or leopard approaches, the elephants flap their ears in warning. Excursions by canoe are also possible, and allow sightseeing of the varied creatures that live in the rivers and on the shores, bordered by dense forests. You must be accompanied by a forest guide in order to see the animals and to move about safely. The park entrance is situated in Motipur. Its headquarters is at Tharkurdwara, 5 mi (8 km) from Chisapani on the Mahendra Raj Marg. There you can hire an elephant and a guide. For safety reasons, moving about in the park at night is prohibited. Be sure to plan your provisions in advance.

The agency, Tiger Tops (Durbar Marg, POB 242, Katmandu), organizes safaris in the parks, particularly in Bardia park.

In Bardia, several wild Asian elephants remain, while those in the other parks of Nepal are domestic, as is the one pictured above.

The bagh chal

One of the traditional games of Nepal is "bagh chal," which can be translated as "move the tigers." It's played on a game board with 25 intersecting points. One of the players has four pieces that represent the tigers, and the other player has 20 pieces that represent the goats. For the tigers, the object of the game is to "devour" the goats; the goats' objective is not to be devoured.

The tigers are set up at the four corners. Players take turns. The goats are placed on the board one by one, and they cannot move until all have been placed. The tigers, on the other hand, can move on every turn, from one point to the next or by "jumping" over a goat to take it out of the game. The goats defend themselves by occupying the intersecting points so that no free points are left for the tigers to occupy. When five goats are lost, the tigers have won. If the goats succeed in surrounding the tigers so none can move, they win.

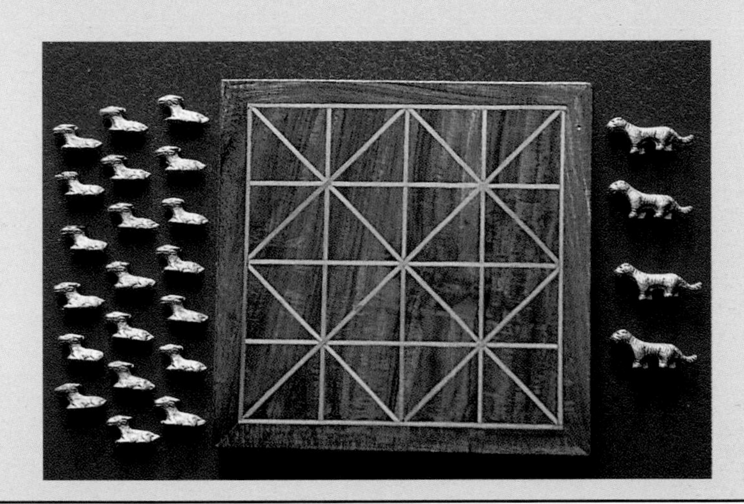

PRACTICAL INFORMATION

The best time to go to the park of Bardia is between September and May.

TRANSPORTATION

■ **BY PLANE.** Flights from Paris arrive in Katmandou by the Tribhuvan airport. Flights from Katmandou to Napalganj last an hour and a half.

■ **BY CAR.** From Katmandou, take the Mahendra Raj Marg to Nepalganj. From Nepalganj, plan on a two-and-a-half-hour drive to the park of Bardia.

CLIMATE

Temperatures: maximum from 72°–77° F (23°– 25° C) (December to February) to 98°–102° F (37°–39° C) (April to June); minimum 46°–48° F (8°–9° C) (December and January) to 80°–81° F (26°–27° C) (June and July). The monsoon season lasts from June to September (6 to 13 in/month) (155 to 325 mm/month); rains are light in November and December less than 2 tenths of an in/month (7-8 mm/month). The most hours of sun occur March to May (nine to ten hours a day) and the least July to August (four to five hours a day).

LODGING

No hotels are located inside the park of Bardia, but camping is allowed within certain specific areas. It's also possible to reserve lodges as well as arrange organized visits in Katmandou (on Durbar Marg).

VISITS

In Nepal, you can visit a large number of temples and palaces. Out of all of these monuments, you must see the Golden Door, guarded by two stone lions, on Hanuman Dhoka square in Katmandou. You can also go to Bhadgaon (or Bhaktapur), 14 mi east of Katmandou, where you can find the superb temple of Nyatapola, which was constructed in 1702. The staircase steps are decorated with two elephants, two lions, two griffins, and two goddesses: Baghini (represented as a tiger) and Singhini (represented as a lion).

RECOMMENDATIONS

Heed the rules of safety, that is, don't travel without a guide and don't go out at night.

The Jaguar

(Panthera onca)

GERMAN: jaguar — IN BELIZE: tiger
BRAZILIAN: onça pintada — FRENCH: jaguar
SPANISH: yaguar, jaguar, tigre americano
GUARANI: yaguareté — MAYA: zacbolay
DUTCH: jagoear — PERUVIAN: otorongo
IN SURINAM: penitigri

Description

The jaguar's head is round and is topped by small ears. Its legs are short and powerful, and its tail long. Its strong jaws and long canines give it a powerful bite. It's probably the most powerful of the cats, although it's not the largest. Its fur ranges from gold to red; and black spots are strewn over head and legs. Rosettes decorate the back and flanks; the rosettes often have one or two smaller spots in their centers. The underbelly is whitish spotted with black. A row of black spots extends the length of the spine, sometimes in a solid line. Melanistic forms exist, on which the spots are still visible.

Measurements. The jaguar's size varies according to geographic origin, with the largest, heaviest individuals weighing up to 99 lb (up to 136 kg), found in the Pantanal in Brazil. Jaguars are larger in forest environments than they are in prairie regions. Weight is approximately 120 lb (55 kg) for males and 80 lb (36 kg) for females. At birth, the young weigh 1½–2 lb (680–990 g). The head and body length is from 44–74 in (112–185 cm) and the tail measures 18–30 in (45–75 cm).

Lifespan. They live up to 20 years in captivity.

Locomotion

The jaguar is a good climber and often rests in tree branches, but it is thought that it usually hunts on the ground. It is an excellent swimmer and can cross rivers.

The jaguar is probably the most powerful of the cats, and is the only one that will attack large reptiles such as snakes, caymans, and tortoises.

Activity

By day, the jaguar usually remains under cover. It rarely ventures into the open, and then only at night. The movements of its prey dictate the jaguar's activity, and therefore the jaguar's activity varies according to the habitat. In the Pantanal in Brazil, jaguars hunt more often during the day, while in Belize, they are more active at night.

Diet

The jaguar's prey is varied: capybaras, peccaries, pacas, deer, spider monkeys, various small mammals, caymans, lizards, snakes, and frequently tortoises whose shells they break with their strong jaws. The jaguar is an opportunist, hunting whatever is available. It also feeds on fish, and even on some kinds of fruit. It prowls the banks of watercourses in search of prey. It often eats monkeys. It is thought that the jaguar doesn't hunt them in the trees, but rather catches them when they forage for food on the ground. Once prey is sighted, the jaguar immediately charges. Usually, the jaguar kills by grasping the prey's head with its teeth and piercing its skull. Little else is known about the jaguar's methods of finding and catching prey. What researchers have learned has been deduced from the tracks and remains, since the jaguar's hunting habits have rarely been observed in the wild.

Predators

None, except humans. However, the young can become prey to various carnivores.

Social behavior

The jaguar is a solitary animal. The size of its territory varies, depending on available prey and human intrusion. Females' territories may overlap; males' territories do not. A male's territory includes that of several females. Not much is known about jaguar behavior because researchers have done few radio tracking experiments on the species. The jaguar's habitat is difficult to reach.

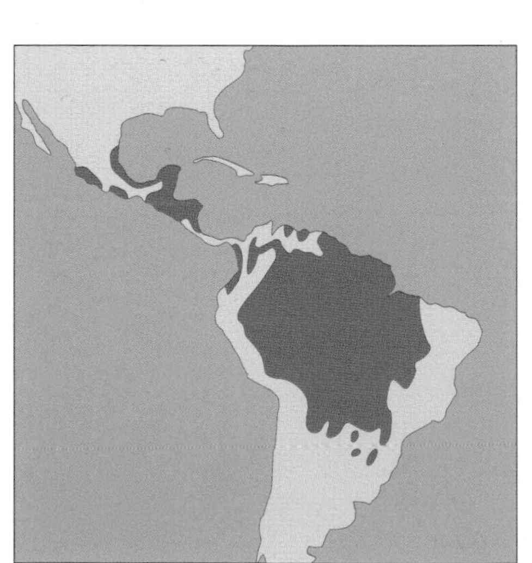

Reproduction

Jaguars have no set reproductive season. Gestation lasts from 98 to 109 days, and while litters can include from one to four newborns, most often two cubs are produced. The cubs open their eyes one to three days after birth, and begin to take solid food at approximately 70 days. The cubs are weaned around 22 weeks of age. Young jaguars remain with their mothers for approximately two years.

Range

Jaguars usually live in damp habitats, such as swampy prairies or dense forests bordering watercourses. They can frequent drier environments if rivers are present, and are found at altitudes up to more than a mile high (2,000 m). Jaguars live in the following countries: Argentina, Belize, Bolivia, Brazil, Colombia, Costa Rica, Ecuador, El Salvador, Guyana, French Guyana, Guatemala, Honduras, Mexico, Nicaragua, Panama, Paraguay, Peru, Surinam, and Venezuela.

Status

Outside the Amazon rain forest, the jaguar population is constantly decreasing practically everywhere it exists. The jaguar has been exterminated from the driest parts of its range in the United States and Mexico, and the grassland areas in Argentina and Paraguay. The sectioning off and destruction of its habitat make it vulnerable. More and more of its habitat is being claimed for agriculture. Jaguars are also killed by farmers and cattle ranchers, who do not want them on their lands. As jaguars do not avoid humans, they are more easily killed than the cautious puma that still survives in areas from which the jaguar has been exterminated.

Historical overview

In the past, the jaguar could be found on both American continents between the latitudes of approximately 35 degrees North and South. Cold and altitude limit its range. Today's jaguar, confined to areas of dense forest, is physically smaller than the jaguar formerly found in the United States.

Until the 1960s, the jaguar was hunted for its fur. The Convention on International Trade in Endangered Species (CITES) has effectively decreased this hunting, although poaching still occurs. Human pressure has caused a constant decrease in the jaguar population, which competes with hunters, ranchers, and farmers. The jaguar's prey is itself hunted and its numbers are decreasing, forcing the jaguar to feed on cattle.

Naturalists use the spots on the jaguar's face to recognize individuals. Due to the inaccessibility of the jaguar's habitat, only radio tracking can provide information on the jaguar's behavior, which remains poorly understood.

Observation site

Brazil (Mato Grosso): Pantanal

The Pantanal is a vast swamp of 92,000 sq mi (230,000 sq km) in the center of South America, straddling three countries — Brazil, Bolivia, and Paraguay. At an altitude of between 110 and 220 yd (100 and 200 m) above sea level, the Pantanal is bordered by the Serra de Maracaju on the east, the Serra da Bodoquena on the south, the Paraguayan and Bolivian Chaco (steppes) on the west, the Chapada dos Parecis on the north, and the Serra do Roncador on the northeast. Rainwater streams down from the highlands to form the Paraguay river and its tributaries. This is one of the best spots to observe the wildlife of Latin America, since the area is relatively open. Called Terra de Ninguem, or "land of no one," it is sparsely populated and has no cities. The Pantanal is flooded during

The psittacides (parakeets, macaws) are plentiful in Brazil, but some species are now extremely endangered.

the rainy season (October to March), which creates *cordilheiras*, small islands of dry land on which the animals take refuge. The waters are highest in January and February, and begin to recede in March. The Pantanal is crossed by a single road, la Transpantaneira, which leads from Pocone to Porto Jofre, a road passable in an all-terrain vehicle during the dry season. On each side of the road extends the zone protected for the conservation of fauna and flora. Elsewhere, the land belongs to *fazendeiros*, who poach and practice slash-and-burn farming.

The 58 mi (145 km) road makes a good observation site. In this protected area lives the typical wildlife of the South American tropical forest, including the unusual tree-dwelling anteater, the tamandua, as well as the largest rodent in existence, the capybara (or cabiai), that spends its day in the water and comes out at night to graze on the plant life, aquatic and otherwise. The jaguars of the Pantanal hunt tortoise, caymans, and fish, as well as peccaries and tapirs. Well-nourished, these jaguars are twice the size of those of Central America.

Fauna and flora

The wildlife consists of pumas, ocelots, jaguarundies, crab foxes, anteaters, tatoos, tapirs, zebus, and monkeys, including black howler and titi monkeys. Mammals adapted to an aquatic habitat are found in the Pantanal, like the giant Brazilian otter or the marsh deer. Among the 658 species of birds that populate the region, the most common is the jabiru, a large wading bird whose wingspan reaches nearly 10 ft (3 m). You can also find parakeets, macaws, toucans, fisher martins, egrets, ibises, spoonbills, and herons. The reptiles include caymans (called jacares by Brazilians), iguanas, and numerous snakes including the enormous anaconda. When nesting, egrets cover the trees with thousands of white droppings. The rivers and streams are home to more than 230 species of fish, including the infamous Piranha. One of the most amazing fish is the dipneumonan *Lepidosiren*, a lunged fish that can survive on dry land.

Among the Pantanal's diverse plant life are trees called ipe, numerous orchids, water hyacinths, and palm trees.

Observation

You must go during the dry season (April through October), but the best time is mid-July to mid-September. Jaguars usually sleep near water, and you are more likely to see them in the early morning when they are resting on the steep riverbanks. Wildlife viewing is best done in a vehicle on the Transpantaneira. The fauna is abundant on the prairies situated 6–12 mi (10–20 km) from Porto Jofre. Ideally, leave Cuiaba very

The Pantanal is entirely flooded from October to March and is inaccessible then. Caymans, called jacares locally, are very numerous everywhere in the Pantanal.

early (around 4:00 A.M.), so you can arrive at Pocone by sunrise, and then spend the day on the road to Porto Jofre.

The best viewing is by boat, since jaguars are usually seen near the watercourses. Boats can be rented in the Pantanal. Leave very early in the morning, preferably before sunrise, to see jaguars sleeping on branches overhanging the streams or prowling along the banks. It's not uncommon to come across paw prints or the remains of a meal. Prey is abundant and jaguars often abandon half-eaten carcasses. You can hire a guide, but it's important to make sure he belongs to the Association of Guides, and to meet him before leaving on the trip. Be sure to bring a pair of binoculars or a spotting scope for the best viewing.

Cuiaba and the gold rush

In 1719, Pascoal Moreira Cabral, a Paulist (an inhabitant of Sao Paulo), found gold when he was hunting Indians along the Cuiaba river. This discovery caused a gold rush. It wasn't easy to reach the region from Sao Paolo, and it took about five months of travel to cover the 1,800 mi (3,000 km) of rivers and streams that led there. Food was rare, and the heat, mosquitoes, and disease often got the best of the *garimpeiros* who attempted the trip in search of fortune. Once a year, miners and black slaves, escorted by soldiers, would depart by canoe to search for the precious metal. The expeditions, which usually included several hundred people, frequently failed. When the gold rush ended, Cuiaba did not disappear from the map, since the region was favorable for cultivation, and the Cuiaba river overflowed with fish. The region continued to attract a few gold seekers; indeed, some still come today to try their luck.

To reach the Cuiaba river, the Portuguese crossed the lands of various tribes of Indians, including the fearsome warriors the Caiapos, the Bororos of the Pantanal, the Parecis who were reduced to slavery in the mines, the Paiagas who resisted the Portuguese, and the Guaicurus, also warriors and good equestrians. These tribes were decimated or reduced to slavery until around the middle of the eighteenth century. Only a few tribes have survived north of the Mato Grosso, like the Erikbatsas, Nhambikuraas, and Cayabis. Indians are also found in the Aripuana and Xingu parks, but the Bororos is the last Indian tribe still able to live off hunting and fishing. In the nineteenth century, the city of Cuiaba became the first Portuguese colony of western Brazil and the third city in the country. Today, with its 285,000 inhabitants, it is the capital of Mato Grosso, which is a mining, agricultural, and timbering state.

PRACTICAL INFORMATION

The best time to go to the Pantanal is between mid-July and mid-September.

TRANSPORTATION

■ **BY PLANE.** Regular flights fly between the United States and Rio de Janeiro. From there you need to get to Cuiaba (Mato Grosso) or to Corumba (mato Grosso do Sul). Flights for these two cities leave from the various large cities of Brazil.

■ **BY CAR.** Cars can be rented at the Cuiaba airport and you can travel by car to Pocone (two hours) to get to the Transpantaneira. No organized transportation is available on site.

CLIMATE

Temperatures fluctuate between 59°–62° F (15°–22° C) and 86°–92° F (29°–33° C) all year long. The maximum rainfall falls between October and April .8–4 in/month (22–105 mm/month) and the minimum between June and August .3–1 in/month (9–27 mm/month). The area gets four to seven hours of sunlight per day.

LODGING

Porto Jofre has a hotel; you can also camp at St. Nicolo's (near the river). In Corumba, you can obtain information on lodging in the *fazendas* (rustic hotels), and renting boats and horses. To the north, several *fazendas* are found off the Transpantaneira.

VISITS

In Cuiaba, the museo do Indio allows you to learn about the lives of the Xavantes, Bororos, and Karajas tribes. It is located within the university Avenida Fernando Correira da Costa.

RECOMMENDATIONS

Bring long-sleeved shirts and long pants, mosquito repellent, and sun protection.

Observation site

Belize: Cockscomb Basin

Formerly called British Honduras, Belize is a veritable natural paradise. Thanks to Peter Wallace, a Scottish pirate, the Europeans discovered the area in 1638. This small country is known especially for its coral reef, one of the most beautiful in the world. More than two-thirds of Belize is covered by tropical forests. A mountain range, the Monts Mayas, crosses the country from northeast to southwest. The rivers and streams flow from these mountains. Elsewhere, the country alternates between swamps and savannas, while the banks of the waterways are bordered with dense forests. Mangroves occupy a large part of the shoreline. Belize is an untouched country whose environment, including 80 percent of its tropical forest, has been preserved.

Inhabited in the past by the Mayas, then by the Karibs, the Mosquitos, and the Lacandons, Belize was colonized by Europeans who brought black slaves.

In 1984, the virgin sanctuary of Cockscomb Basin, in the southern portion of Belize near Dangriga, became the first preserve in the world dedicated to the protection of the jaguar. The creation of this preserve is largely due to the efforts of Alan Rabinowitz, who was devoted to the feline. He managed to equip jaguars with radio collars, better to understand the species' biology.

The Cockscomb Basin is shallow and bordered by forests. It is found in a hollow between sharp mountains that culminate in Victoria Peak, the highest point in the country. In 1990, the preserve was expanded to 164 sq mi (41,000 hectares). The area has become a sanctuary for wildlife in order to protect the cat species that live there: jaguars, pumas, jaguarundis, ocelots, and margays.

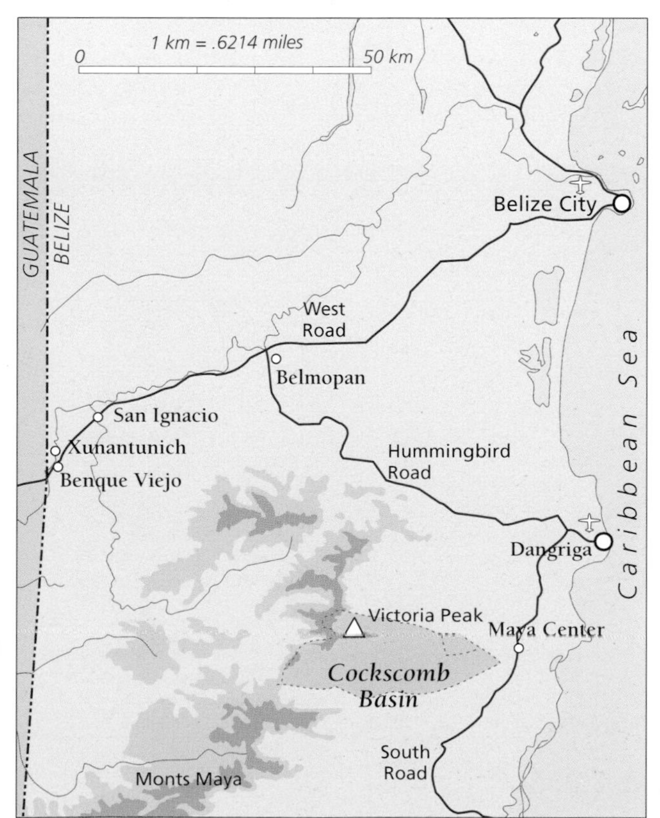

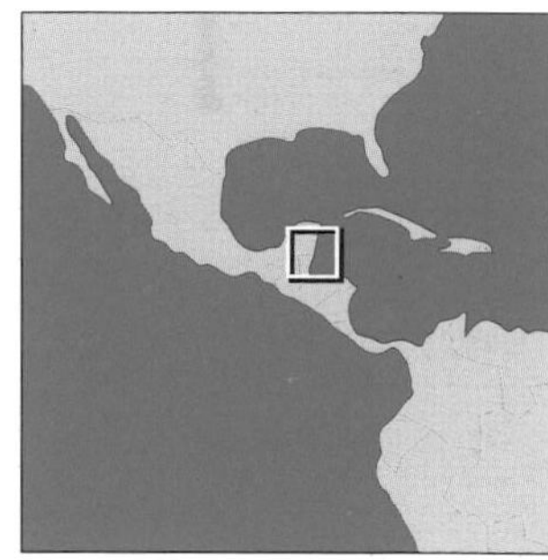

Fauna and flora

In Belize, 4,000 species of flowering plants, 700 species of trees, and 530 of birds have been counted, including toucans, macaws, scarlet macaws, agami herons, aracaris, great hoccos, and ocellated turkeys. This region also shelters numerous mammals: pumas, ocelots, jaguarundis, and margays, tapirs, howler monkeys, spider monkeys, coatis, kinkajous, among many others. Extraordinary frogs such as peepers and dendrobatids, whose venom is used to poison Indian arrow points, also live here, each sporting colors more vivid than the next. This region is inhabited by numerous snakes such as various species of boas, fer-de-lances, and coral snakes.

Belize has remained largely uncultivated and has retained about 80% of its tropical forests. The fauna is rich, with numerous species still to be discovered.

PRACTICAL INFORMATION

The best time to go to Belize is between February and April.

TRANSPORTATION

■ **BY PLANE.** From Paris, flights for Belize City make a stop in Mexico, Guatemala, or Florida. Plan on seven to eight hours to Miami and two to three hours to Belize City.

■ **BY CAR.** You can rent a car in Belize City and go to Dangriga (Stann Creek district), then take the Southern highway to Maya Center Village, which is the office of the preserve. The entrance to the park is located 6 1/2 miles (11 km) to the west.

CLIMATE

The climate is very damp; cyclones are frequent in October. Temperatures range between 66°–77° F (19°–24° C) and 80°–88° F (27°–31° C). The maximum rain falls between May and January 4–12 in/month (110–305 mm/month) and the minimum between February and April 1.5 in/month (40 mm/month).

LODGING

You can sleep under a tent, or in a dormitory next to the visitors' center at Cockscomb Park. Reservations are recommended at the Belize Audubon Society (see the next page), especially between November and April.

VISITS

Belize is also a popular spot for scuba diving. The coral barrier teems with life, and the atolls (islands of coral that enclose lagoons) near shore are worth the stop. Don't miss the Maya site of Xunantunish; from Dangriga, take Hummingbird Highway to Belmopan, then continue west toward San Ignacio. About 2.4 mi (4 km) before Benque Viejo, at San Jose Succotz, a road leads to the site. Chichen Itza in Mexico, in the center of the Yucatan, on the Merida - Valladolid - Cancun road, includes illustrations of jaguars.

RECOMMENDATIONS

Anti-malaria treatment is a must, and before leaving you must get the mandatory vaccinations. Check beforehand to find out what is required. Avoid snakes, particularly the deadly fer-de-lance and coral varieties. Bring insect protection and warm clothing, as the nights can be cool.

The forests consist of cashews, mahoganies, cedars, pines, rosewood, resin trees, and gums.

Observation

The best time to go to Belize is between February and April. Don't visit during the rainy season, from May to January. The observation of cats, particularly the jaguar, can be done on the shores of the rivers of the Cockscomb Basin with a local guide. Most often, only signs of them can be found, such as claw marks or paw prints on the ground, but with luck you can spot a jaguar in the shelter of the dense forests. Sometimes it roams at dusk or dawn, but during the day, the jaguar most often rests on a branch of the bordering trees. Get to the observation spots early in the morning, and be quiet so your movements won't cause the animals to beat a hasty retreat. Take your time looking at the branches above the steep riverbanks or at the banks themselves. Jaguar leftovers can often be seen, such as crushed tortoise shells. The cat removes the top of the land turtle's shell, then enlarges the hole to get at the snack inside. However, it breaks open the shells of aquatic turtles from the side. The jaguar is the only animal that will attack caymans, which it kills with a bite to the neck, and then tears into the animal's flanks. In the forest, it often consumes its prey entirely (peccaries, for example), and leaves no trace.

Coatis are, like raccoons, members of the *Procyonidae* family.

Information about the country's preserves is available through the Belize Audubon Society, 49 Southern Foreshore, Belize City. Information can also be gotten from the Tourist Office, 83 Front Street, Belize City. A guide is necessary. This is not a good place to get lost, and spotting the signs of jaguars and other animals is tricky. Leave the leadership to an expert.

The jaguar in Native Indian civilization

The jaguar is an integral feature of the beliefs of native South American Indians who made sculptures and drawings of the cat, which can be found in Chichen Itza, most notably. Among the Olmecs, the Mayas, and the Aztecs, the jaguar was pivotal in their cultures. The jaguar, portrayed with childlike features, symbolized power. Immense monuments were dedicated to the jaguar cult. Aztec kings were considered the descendants of Tezcatlipoca, the jaguar god. Mayan warriors would go into combat dressed in the skins, claws, and fangs of the jaguar. When they hunted the cat, they begged forgiveness from the gods. Their priests were given the title "balam," which means "jaguar." The jaguar, an emblem of fear and death, figured as well on funereal vases.

In Mexico, the Indians thought that humans could change into jaguars. The Totonacs believed that clay objects could be transformed into jaguars. As for the Nahuas, they thought the spotted coat of the feline gave physical form to the sky and its constellations.

The Arawak Indians of South America have kept their rituals to metamorphose into jaguars, which gives the shamans the power to attract good and evil. The Pantaneiros in the Pantanal in Brazil still think that eating jaguar meat develops the strength and virility necessary to be a good *zagaeiro*, or jaguar hunter. The *zagaeiros* hunt the jaguar with a wooden lance tipped with metal. The hunter follows the jaguar to the foot of a tree, and provokes the cat to attack him; he then thrusts the end of the lance in the ground, and the jaguar impales itself when it leaps on the man.

The Puma, or Cougar

(Puma concolor)

GERMAN: puma, berglöwe, silberlöwe, kaguar — IN BELIZE: red tiger — BRAZILIAN: onca vermmelha — SPANISH: puma, leon americano, coguardo — GUARANI: guasura, yagua-pyta — MAYA: cabcoh — DUTCH: poema – IN SURINAM: poema, redi-tigri — FRENCH: puma

Description

The puma's body and neck are long; its head is small and its ears short and round. The tail is long. The fur color varies from gray-blue to red-brown. The latter color is more frequent in tropical areas. Pumas living in the north are more often gray. The puma has no spots. The tip of the muzzle and the underbelly are white or cream-colored. Sometimes melanistic forms occur.

Size varies with geographic region. The largest pumas are found in the southern and northern range extremes. Pumas from mountainous regions also are larger than those that live on the plains. Of the large cats, the puma has the greatest difference in length between its hind and front legs; the hind legs are longer, which makes the puma an excellent jumper.

Measurements. Male head and body length: 42–78 (105–195 cm); female 38–60 (96–151 cm); tail from 21–32 in (53–81 cm). Males weigh from 147–226 lb (67–103 kg); females from 79–132 lb (36–60 kg) and newborns weigh 20 oz (500 g).
Lifespan. The puma lives up to 18 years in captivity.

Locomotion

The puma can perform a standing jump of up to 7.7 yd (7 m) in height, and can also jump from tree to tree. Its jumping ability allows it to live comfortably in the most irregular, craggy terrains.

Activity

Pumas can be active day and night. They adapt to their prey's periods of activity. Those who live in the mountains hunt by day, while the pumas of the plains are usually nocturnal. Pumas are very cautious and difficult to spot.

Diet

Essentially, pumas feed on members of the deer family, like elk; but depending on the region, also on wild pigs, opossums, raccoons, beavers, porcupines, pacas, agoutis, bats, and lizards. In the southern parts of their range, their large prey are guanacos and rheas rather than deer. They can kill prey several times their size, such as elans. The prey's size depends on what is available since pumas are opportunistic hunters. They eat what's within their reach.

When a puma spots potential prey, it quietly approaches, remaining hidden as long as possible, then charges and kills it with a bite to the neck. Generally, it doesn't give chase. The puma drags the body to a sheltered place to eat, and sometimes conserves the remains by covering it with vegetation or snow.

Predators

The puma has no predators except humans. However, since it hunts large prey, it can be killed during its attacks. Male pumas sometimes eat the young of their own species, who can also be the victims of various predators.

Social Behavior

The puma is a solitary cat. The territories of females often overlap, and in turn are overlapped by the territory of males. The more female territories a male's territory overlaps, the better his chances of reproduction. The territories of males do not overlap, but other males and young pumas may pass through the territory without injury, as long as they move on and don't try to establish themselves. Pumas must hold large territories to find enough food. In mountainous regions, they must move down into the canyons during the winter, following their prey to greener pastures.

Pumas do not communicate through loud roars as do the other large cats. This is due to the construction of the hyoid bones that connect the larynx with the skull. Most

Deer is the puma's preferred prey, but puma also eat various small vertebrates. In South America, large prey includes guanacos (cousins of the llama) and rheas, large running birds.

large cats have hyoid bones which allows the vocal apparatus to move freely and produce roaring sounds. In small cats, the hyoid bone is fully ossified and rigid, and this prevents that full-throated roar. Although the puma is as large as the leopard, it shares this hyoid bone construction with the small cats, and therefore cannot roar.

Pumas mark their territory by scratching trees and other upright objects, by leaving uncovered feces, and by spraying urine. These marks tell any intruder that this territory is taken.

Reproduction

For pumas, no set reproductive season exists. During the mating period, males and females hunt and sleep together. Gestation lasts approximately 90 days; litters generally include one to four young but most often three. The female raises her young alone. The cub's fur is flecked, which helps camouflage the young in a nest of leaves, a rocky cavity, or a thicket. Cubs begin to eat meat at 6 weeks of age, but nursing lasts more than three months. At several months of age, they tag along and help eat the prey their mother has killed. They are independent at around 2 years of age, but brothers and sisters will sometimes remain together for several months.

Range

Pumas live in forests, mountains, irregular terrain, swamps, prairies, and brush, and can live at altitudes up to 2.8 mi (4,500 m). They are found in western Canada and in the United States west of the Rockies, in the southern part of Florida, and in Central and South America. Of all the cats, the puma has a range that extends the farthest in latitude, going from the Yukon in Canada to the strait of Magellan. They can be found in the following countries: Argentina, Belize, Bolivia, Brazil, Canada, Chile, Colombia, Costa Rica, Ecuador, El Salvador, Honduras, Guatemala, Guyana, Mexico, Nicaragua, Panama, Paraguay, Peru, Surinam, the United States, and Venezuela.

Status

The species as a whole is not endangered, but the Florida subspecies is threatened with extinction. Its range has dwindled and now only several dozen Florida pumas remain, living in the southern part of the state. The eastern puma (subspecies *cougar*) has disappeared since the early part of this century due to deforestation, the reduction in its prey, and hunting. Since then, sightings of the eastern puma in the eastern United States have been reported, but no real proof of its existence has been presented. If these sightings are true, no more than 50 individuals could still exist. According to some experts, these sightings are probably animals released by people who had taken them as pets, and abandoned them when they became adults. Pumas raised in captivity adapt fairly well to life in the wild. The redevelopment of forests and the increase in potential prey in the eastern U.S. suggest that pumas may have readapted to this part of the country.

The situation in Central and South America is better than in the North, and the puma still lives where the jaguar had already disappeared. Still, the local populations have the tendency to consider pumas

harmful animals and a threat to cattle. The status of the puma in Central and South America is not well known because access is difficult in the regions where it lives, and because the puma is very cautious around humans.

Historical overview

Pumas avoid men, and few attacks on humans have been reported. The first American colonists did not view the puma as being as harmful an animal as they did the wolf, for example. The gauchos even called it "Amigo del christiano" (friend of the Christian). Nevertheless, pumas sometimes kill cattle. They are afraid of dogs and are easy to trap and kill. This is why trapping, poisoning, and sport hunting, in addition to the destruction of its habitat and decrease of its prey, rapidly eliminated the puma from many regions. For a long time, the puma had a price on its head. In 1959 in New Brunswick, a puma skin was worth $20. Beginning in the mid-1960s, puma hunting was prohibited in some U.S. states, but the puma had already been exterminated in the East, except in Florida.

The puma is very cunning and cautious. Since its experiences with humans have been so negative, it has moved to areas far away from all human activity. As a result, observing it is difficult, and until recently, zoologists knew little about its biology. Since the work of Hornecker in 1964, researchers have conducted successive studies on the puma, but much remains to be learned about the cat that Theodore Roosevelt named the "lord of fugitive murder."

It was on his fourth voyage, that Christopher Columbus saw his first puma, which he took for a lion. Since the puma attacked humans only very rarely, the first Europeans did not hunt it right away. However, the puma quickly became the object of persecution, because it was accused of killing cattle. "Sport" hunting eliminated many pumas, particularly from the eastern United States where it has since disappeared.

Observation site

United States (the Rocky Mountains): Bryce Canyon (Utah)

In the United States, the Rocky Mountains have become a refuge for many animal species. The Rocky Mountains extend for more than 2,880 mi (4,800 km) from Canada to Mexico, with peaks reaching 10,000 ft (3,000 m) in the north and up to 13,333 ft (4,000 m) in the south. The mountains provide a variety of habitats, and therefore a diversity of plant and wildlife has been preserved, due in part to the inaccessibility of the habitats. At 60 million years of age, the Rockies are young in geological terms, and indeed, their plant life is less diversified than that of, say, the Appalachians. The western watershed is characterized by conifer forests; the eastern watershed is more arid, wooded only at the higher elevations. The Rockies provide a good habitat for the puma, which has practically totally disappeared east of that range except in Florida. Early in the twentieth century in the West, deforestation and reduction of prey animals greatly decreased their numbers. However, due to hunting bans, their numbers are increasing. Although still threatened, they are now fairly common in the West. For example, the puma population has increased so much in California that a recent bill was put before the voters to allow sport hunting of the cats again. Fortunately, the bill was defeated.

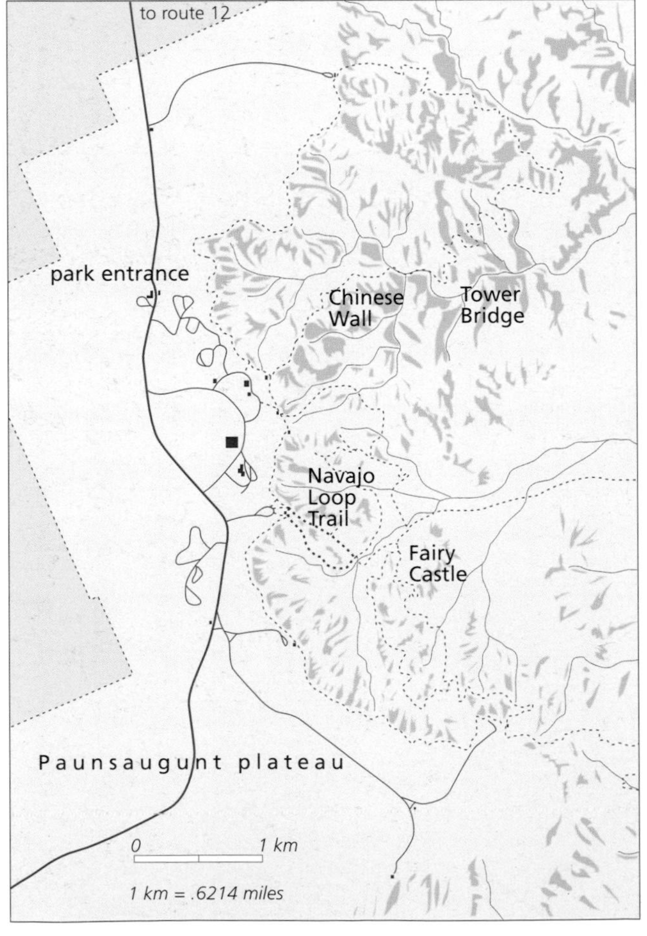

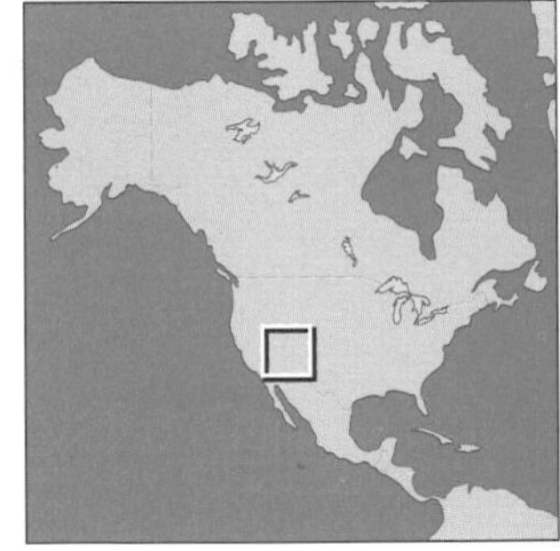

In 1872, a protected area was established in the Yellowstone area. This event marked the beginning of an awareness of the need for nature conservation. In 1916, a park system was created in the U.S., and today the national parks number 340. Bryce Canyon Park and Canyonlands Park, both in the Rockies in Utah, give you your best chance of spotting pumas.

Located in the midsection of the range, or the "Middle Rockies," Bryce Canyon Park extends for 58 sq mi (146 sq km). It consists of a group of canyons hollowed in the limestone plateau of the Paunsaugunt (native American for "land of beavers"). Here erosion has carved soaring, fortress-like sculptures out of the rock, in colors from white to ocher. You can enjoy the magnificent panorama by taking Rim Drive around the park.

Fauna and flora

The Rockies are remarkable for their wildlife, which includes deer, elk, pronghorn antelope, elands, grizzly bears, bison, porcupines, foxes, coyotes, lynx, raccoons, beavers, rabbits, and many small rodents. Some 164 bird species inhabit the park, including the bald eagle, the United States' national bird since 1782.

Junipers, ponderosa pines, and firs comprise the principal flora of the region.

Observation

You can visit the Rockies practically all year but at certain times the cold and snow make access difficult. The best time is May through

Bryce Canyon consists of irregular and difficult-to-reach terrain, frequented by pumas.

October, although it's best to avoid July and August when tourism is at its peak and daytime temperatures are very high.

Throughout the year, pumas are active at night and sometimes through midmorning. In summer, they also come out during the day. Usually lizards and squirrels are the only animals out and about during the day, but at twilight and dawn a richer fauna can be seen. Hiking or horseback riding are the best ways to explore the mountains, since it's easier to catch the animals unaware. Marked trails, like the Navajo Loop Trail, are maintained for hiking and riding. Pumas are extremely shy, and even traces of their presence are often difficult to find. If you're lucky, however, you may see one, even in the summer at midday. They generally live in the least accessible areas. However, they move around a great deal in search of food. Occasionally surprised visitors find themselves followed by one of these "mountain lions." These meetings are rarely dangerous; however, it's not unheard of for pumas to attack humans. Above all, don't turn and run from the cat; you don't want to act like prey. Instead, stand still, maintain eye contact, and most likely the puma will go on its way.

A nature guide is helpful when you are exploring the park. The steep, rocky areas that the puma calls home can be difficult to reach.

Prairie dogs and squirrels are everywhere and are easy to observe.

In some areas, the elk is one of the puma's favorite prey.

The puma and the Native Americans

The Central American Indians devoted a cult to the jaguar, and the Native Americans of North America and the Andes venerated the puma. The ancient Peruvian city of Cuzco was arranged in the form of the cat. Moreover, the word "puma" comes from quechua.

Many Native Americans thought that the puma was a marine panther who reigned over the aquatic world and controlled storms. Certain Indian legends attribute human behavior to animals, particularly the puma. The Indians thought it was the puma who, while trying to devour the moon or the sun, created eclipses. The Tupis called the puma "cuguacuara," the word from which cougar is derived. In New Mexico, the Cochites sculpted two life-size pumas out of rock for an altar still used today by certain Native Americans. Zuni hunters carried with them small stone pumas.

For the Native Americans of California, the puma was a god who furnished them a good portion of their food. Vultures and condors guided them to the cougar's prey. Some Native Americans of South America and North America ate puma meat. For example, the Indians of the Olympic mountains in Washington used the puma's fur and hide for various purposes. A sheath for arrows and a quiver made of puma skin was found among the Navajos.

For a long time, the European settlers stifled Native American culture, to say the least. Today, a revival of the Native American culture and heritage has begun.

PRACTICAL INFORMATION

The best time to visit Bryce Canyon is between May and October.

TRANSPORTATION

■ BY PLANE. Take a flight to Salt Lake City from the American city closest to you. From there, fly to Cedar City and catch a bus to Bryce Canyon Park.

■ BY CAR. From Salt Lake City, take Highway 15 to reach Cedar City, then continue on to Bryce Canyon.

CLIMATE

In the Rockies, the winters are cold and dry, and the summer days and nights have great extremes in temperature. At low altitudes, it can be very hot. In July and August in Bryce Canyon, the average daytime temperature is at least 80° F (27° C) and at night the temperature is 46° F (7° C). In December and January, temperatures drop to below 32° F (0° C). The rainfall is from .5–1.8 in (13–45 mm) per month throughout the year. The hours of daylight are longest from May to August (11–13 hours per day) and shortest in December and January (four hours a day).

LODGING

Various hotels are found in the park and during the summer camping sites are available. Water is provided. Camping in the wild is permitted.

VISITS

From Rim Drive (a cliff-side road) in Bryce Canyon Park, you can see Bryce Amphitheater and Bryce Point. The lookouts over the rock formations of Tower Bridge, Chinese Wall, and Fairy Castle are exceptionally lovely. Don't miss Lake Powell, several miles south of the park next to Page, Arizona. Enormous red cliffs loom over the water. To explore it more easily, rent a small boat.

RECOMMENDATIONS

Given the fluctuations in temperature between day and night, bring summer clothes for the days and long pants, jackets, and warm shirts for the evenings.

APPENDIX

Protection of felines

Today, cats are still abundantly hunted, either because they threaten livestock and more rarely humans, or for their fur. Trade in feline skins is very active today, and for that reason numerous species are threatened despite protection programs.

Protection of cat species must be combined with conservation of the environment and cannot take place without also improving the standard of living of local human populations. The latter must participate in protective measures, and be included in the tourism which accompanies the creation of preserves. Their exclusion often poses a problem in countries where poverty is great, as the creation of preserves creates a shortage of lands for cultivation or raising animals.

Cheetahs are among the most threatened cats. They are often so disturbed by tourists that they hunt during the hottest hours of the day, at the time when humans take refuge in the shade.

Enclosing parks is also problematic, because it prevents the natural movements of animal populations and brings about epidemics. Management of park wildlife is a complicated issue. The special circumstances the parks create can bring about population imbalances in the park's species. Because of this, the veterinarians of Etosha Park have administered a contraceptive pill to lionesses to limit the proliferation of the species.

The American parks are often cited as good examples of proper wildlife management; however, the parks have substantial financial support and cannot be compared to the parks of countries that do not have the financial means. The development of tourism in the parks is beneficial to the protection of the natural environment, but excess tourism brings about the reverse effect. For example, in 1994 American parks welcomed 270 million visitors. In Yellowstone National Park, the visitors were so numerous and foolhardy that it became necessary to move the bears away from them. On the other hand, thanks to the success of such parks, the National Parks Service is collaborating in the creation and maintenance of parks in approximately ninety countries.

In places where wild lands are scarce, such as in Europe, space for large predators is virtually no longer available. The proximity of these carnivores creates fear, and the public's opinion of their presence is not very favorable. That is why it is necessary to inform and educate the public about the need to protect the wilderness and to respect and understand its inhabitants.

Current techniques of insemination and of embryonic transfer are the tools that may allow us to save species that are endangered and no longer genetically diverse due to lack of contact between very distant populations. These techniques will allow the increase of wild populations, but also will permit us to assure the reproduction of captive animals by maintaining the genetic diversity of the species, indispensable to their survival. Unfortunately, in many cases, animals born in captivity will never be returned to their natural environment, either because they lack the ability to survive or because the environment is too degraded.

Status of the feline species

The red list of the UICN (International Union for the Conservation of Nature) defines species in immediate danger, endangered, vulnerable, rare, somewhat threatened, and status unknown. CITES (Convention on International Trade in Endangered Species) classification in Appendix I defines rare or endangered species in which trade for commercial ends is not permitted. Appendix II defines species that are not rare or endangered but could become so if trade were not regulated.

SPECIES	UICN	CITES
Bobcat *(Lynx rufus)*	Somewhat threatened	Appendix II
Caracal *(Caracal caracal)*	Somewhat threatened	Appendix I & II
Black-footed cat *(Felis nigripes)*	Somewhat threatened	—
Flat-headed cat *(Prionailurus planiceps)*	Vulnerable	Appendix I
Geoffrey's cat *(Felis geoffroyi)*	Somewhat threatened	Appendix II
Jungle cat *(Felis chaus)*	Somewhat threatened	—
Iriomote cat *(Prionailurus iriomotensis)*	Endangered	Appendix II
Sand cat *(Felis margarita)*	Somewhat threatened	Appendix II
SUBSPECIES: Pakistani cat *(Felis margarita scheffeli)*	Rare	—
Pallas's cat *(Felis manul)*	Somewhat threatened	Appendix II
SUBSPECIES: *Felis manul ferrigineous*	Rare	—
Andes cat *(Felis jacobitus)*	Vulnerable	Appendix I
Pampas cat *(Felis colocolo)*	Somewhat threatened	—
African golden cat *(Felis aurata)*	Somewhat threatened	—
Asian golden cat *(Felis temmincki)*	Rare	Appendix II
Borneo golden cat *(Felis badia)*	Vulnerable	Appendix II
Bengal cat *(Prionailurus bengalensis)*	Somewhat threatened	Appendix II
certain populations		Appendix I
Chinese desert cat *(Felis bieti)*	Status unknown	—
Philippines leopard cat (not described)	Vulnerable	—
Marbled cat *(Felis marmorata)*	Status unknown	Appendix II
Fishing cat *(Felis viverrinus)*	Rare	Appendix II
Rusty-spotted cat *(Prionailurus rubiginosus)*	Status unknown	—
Wildcat *(Felis sylvestris)*	Somewhat threatened	—
SUBSPECIES: Scottish wildcat *(Felis sylvestris grampia)*	Vulnerable	—
Cheetah *(Acinonyx jubatus)*	Vulnerable	Appendix I
SUBSPECIES: Asian cheetah *(Acinonyx jubatus venaticus)*	In immediate danger	—
Northwest African cheetah *(Acinonyx jubatus hecki)*	Endangered	—
Jaguar *(Panthera onca)*	Rare	Appendix I
Jaguarundi *(Felis yagouaroundi)*	Somewhat threatened	Appendix II
SUBSPECIES: Texas jaguarundi *(Felis yagouaroundi)*	Status unknown	—
Kodkod *(Felis guigna)*	Vulnerable	—

SPECIES	UICN	CITES
Lion *(Panthera leo)*	Vulnerable	Appendix II
SUBSPECIES:		
Asian lion *(Panthera leo persica)*	Endangered	Appendix I
North American lynx *(Lynx canadensis)*	Somewhat threatened	Appendix II
Spanish lynx *(Lynx pardinus)*	Endangered	Appendix II
Eurasian lynx *(Lynx lynx)*	Somewhat threatened	Appendix II
SUBSPECIES:		
Lynx of the Caucasus *(Lynx lynx dinniki)*	Status unknown	—
Margay *(Felis wieddii)*	Rare	Appendix II
SUBSPECIES:		
Felis wieddii salvinia and *Felis wieddii nicaraguae*		Appendix I
Ocelot *(Felis pardalis)* certain populations	Somewhat threatened	Appendix II
SUBSPECIES:		
Texas ocelot *(Felis pardalis albescens)*	Status unknown	—
Snow leopard *(Panthera uncia)*	Endangered	Appendix I
Little spotted cat *(Felis tigrinus)*	Rare	Appendix II
SUBSPECIES:		
Costa Rican oncilla *(Felis tigrinus oncilla)*		Appendix I
Leopard *(Panthera pardus)*	Somewhat threatened	Appendix I
SUBSPECIES:		
North African leopard *(Panthera pardus panthera)*	In immediate danger	—
Anatolian leopard *(Panthera pardus tulliana)*	In immediate danger	—
Arabian leopard *(Panthera pardus nimr)*	In immediate danger	—
Love leopard *(Panthera pardus orientalis)*	In immediate danger	—
Javan leopard *(Panthera pardus melas)*	Endangered	—
Leopard of the Caucasus *(Panthera pardus ciscaucasia)*	Endangered	—
North China leopard *(Panthera pardus japonensis)*	Endangered	—
Sri Lankan leopard *(Panthera pardus kotiya)*	Endangered	—
Clouded leopard *(Neofelis nebulosa)*	Vulnerable	Appendix I
Puma *(Felis concolor)*	Somewhat threatened	Appendix II
SUBSPECIES:		
Florida puma *(Felis concolor coryi)*	In immediate danger	Appendix I
Eastern puma *(Felis concolor cougar)*	In immediate danger	Appendix I
Serval *(Leptailurus serval)*	Somewhat threatened	Appendix II
SUBSPECIES:		
North African serval *(Leptailurus serval constantinus)*	Endangered	—
Tiger *(Panthera tigris)*	Endangered	Annex I
SUBSPECIES:		
Tiger of love *(Panthera tigris altaica)*	In immediate danger	Annex II
South China tiger *(Panthera tigris amoyensisa)*	In immediate danger	—
Sumatran tiger *(Panthera tigris sumatrae)*	In immediate danger	—

Observing felines

Observing wild cats is a difficult thing to do because they are shy animals, often nocturnal, and at times dangerous. Only a few species can be observed in the favorable conditions that natural parks offer.

In fact, in these areas where the animals are protected, a certain density of population is maintained. The park's design also allows for easier observation, and guides are often on site. Moreover, it is important that the animals are not disturbed everywhere; indeed, in preserves, the observers are controlled and guided, which is not the case elsewhere. For all of these reasons, preserves are the preferred places to go to observe wildlife. Moreover, it is often impossible to observe felines outside the park setting, with the exception of Africa, where it is at times as easy to see animals outside the parks as within.

Eurasian felines are very difficult to approach because they are rare and their natural environment is limited; they are very shy and flee humans. This is also often the case with American species.

There is no guarantee that you will be able to observe animals at the sites described in this book, with the exception of Africa. Elsewhere, you will need both patience and luck. You must be able to recognize signs of their presence, and follow certain rules: take into account the animals' hours of activity, do not make noise, and approach the sites where animals are present slowly. Ideally, find a naturalist or guide who knows the site well and the species that you wish to see. It is imperative to be equipped with a pair of binoculars so that you can observe the animals while respecting their privacy and tranquility.

Identifying marks

The paw prints of felines are round, with a triangular heel and four pad prints; the claws do not mark because they are retracted.

Wild animals indicate their presence by leaving leftovers and marking their territory by roars, claw marks on tree trunks, and so on. The agitation of other animals such as monkeys and birds can also indicate the presence of predators. Vultures circling overhead indicates the place where predators devour their kills, on which these scavenger birds are waiting to dine.

Felines abandon the carcasses of large ungulates, but when you find the carcasses, it is impossible to know whether they are the leftovers from felines or from other large predators. Leopards hoist their kills into trees, and it is difficult to see them. Some felines such as the puma hide their prey under the snow in the winter. In some cases, jaguars leave the shells of eviscerated turtles, but many mammals are entirely eaten, without a single trace remaining.

If the presence of tourists is at times invasive, it is preferable to that of hunters with whom the environment was crowded for many years. And if the animals of the parks become accustomed to human presence, it is necessary to ensure that the disturbance is as small as possible.

Respect for natural sites

It is important to avoid off-road travel, which damages natural sites and creates clouds of dust. You must not light fires, nor toss out lighted cigarette butts, and you need to be careful to leave nothing behind. Be mindful that nothing is done which may harm the site and its inhabitants, whether fauna or flora. In natural parks, it is vital to be informed of the regulations and to respect them.

Safety

On safaris, certain rules of safety must be respected. It is safest to travel in an all-terrain vehicle in the African preserves, where the roads are not paved. Speeding is dangerous because of the presence of wildlife. Do not take unnecessary risks trying to approach the animals; bring good binoculars instead. Moreover, close proximity is harmful to the animals' tranquility. If they seem agitated or behave aggressively, move away. You must not get out of or leave your vehicle when wild animals are present. In some preserves, open vehicles are prohibited. Finally, if you encounter a wild animal, avoid fleeing from it because you may appear to it to be prey, which could provoke an attack. Maintain eye contact while facing the animal and call for help or slowly try to reach shelter. Generally, the animal ends up moving off on its own.

Useful addresses

Belize
• Belize Consulate
15 Thayer Street
London W1, Great Britain

Brazil
• Embassy of Brazil
34, cours Albert 1
75008 Paris, France

India
• Indian Office of Tourism
13, Boulevard Haussmann
75009 Paris, France

• Embassy of India
20 rue Alberic-Magnard
75016 Paris, France

Indonesia
• Embassy of Indonesia
49, rue Cortembert
75016 Paris, France

Kenya
• Kenya Tourist Office
5, rue Volney
75002 Paris, France

• Embassy of Kenya
3, rue Cimarosa
75016 Paris, France

Namibia
• Embassy of the Republic of Namibia
80, avenue Foch
75016 Paris, France

Nepal
• Embassy of Nepal
45 bis, rue des Acacias
75017 Paris, France

Senegal
• Embassy of Senegal
14, Avenue Robert-Schumann 75007 Paris

• Senegalese National Tourist Office
15, rue Remuscat
75016 Paris, France

Tanzania
• Embassy of Tanzania
70, Boulevard Pereire
75017 Paris, France

Zimbabwe
• Embassy of Zimbabwe
5, rue de Tilsitt
75008 Paris, France

Organizations

• UICN Cat Specialist Group
1172 Bougy, Switzerland

• WWF-France
B.P. 3030
94944 Créteil cedex 9

Dictionary

English	French	Portuguese/Brazilian	Spanish
bank, side	rive	riba	borde
bedding site	couche	cama	cama
bird	oiseau	passaro	ave
buffalo	buffle	bufalo	bufalo
bush	fourré	espesso	espesura
carrion	charogne	carcaça	carrona
cayman, caïman	caïman	caimao	caiman
cub	bébé (félin)	bebé/nemén	joven
claw	griffe	unha	garra
deer	cerf	cervo	ciervo
dentition	dentition	dentiçao	denticion
fang	croc	prsea	comillo
fasting	jeûne	jejum	ayuno
fore paw	patte avant	pata antes	pata antes
fur	fourrure	pele	piel
guide	guide	guia/vaqueano	guia
hair	poil	pelo	pelo
hare	lièvre	lebre	liebre
hind paw	patte arrière	pata atras	pata atras
home range	répartition	partilha	distribucion
hunting dog	lycaon		
hyena	hyène	hiena	hiena
making noise	faire du bruit	estar ruido	hacer ruido
marking	indice	indicio	indicio
monkey, ape	singe	macaco	mono
nursing	allaitement	aleitamento	amamantamiento
observation	observation	observaçao	observacion
poaching	braconnage	caça furtiva	caza furtiva
predator	prédateur		
prey	proie	presa	presa
print	trace		trazo
rabbit	lapin	coelho	conejo
rodent	rongeur	roedor	roedor
safety	sécurité	segurança	seguridad
scats, droppings	crotte, fèces	excremento	cagarruta
scratch	griffure	arranhar	aranar
territory	territoire	territorio	territorio
to growl	grogner	grunhir	grunir
to purr	ronronner	ronronar	
to roar	rugir	rugir	rugir
to stalk	chasser à l'affût	caçar à espreita	acecho
to surprise	surprendre	surpreender	sorprender
tortoise, turtle	tortue	tartaruga	tortuga
track	piste	pista	pista
trap	piège	armadilha/arapuca	trampa
unpredictable	imprévisible	imprevisto	imprevisible
vulture	vautour	abutre	buitre
wildebeest	gnou		
yearling	juvénile	juvenil	juvenil
zebra	zèbre	zebra	cebra

Glossary

Aeluroids (or feliforms): Group of mammals of the order of carnivores, defined notably by the presence of a septum (or partition) formed of two elements and which divides the tympanic bubble into two chambers. Includes the following families: Hyanidae (hyenas and aardwolf), Felidae (felines), Viverridae (civets and genets), and Herpestidae (mongooses).
Arctoids: Group of mammals of the order of carnivores, defined notably by the presence of an undivided tympanic bubble. Includes the following families: Ursidae (bears and the great panda), Procyonidae (raccoon, coati, etc.), Ailuridae (red panda), and Mustelidae (weasels, otters, martens, badgers).
Binocular vision: Vision utilizing both eyes, in which the fields of vision overlap.
Biotope: Defined place serving as an environment to a community of species.
Caniforms: Group of mammals in the order of carnivores defined by the presence of an undivided (arctoids) or partially divided (Canidae) tympanic bubble.
Carnassials: Jugal teeth (fourth upper premolar and first lower molar) having a characteristic form unique to members of the order of carnivores. These teeth have a developed cutting zone; that of the lower carnassial and upper carnassial function like the two blades of a pair of scissors. The grinding portion of these teeth is reduced or absent.
Feliforms: See aeluroids.
Hyoid bone: An apparatus formed by a series of cartilaginous or partially ossified elements and situated at the level of the pharynx.
IUCN (International Union for the Conservation of Nature): Organization grouping specialists responsible for defining the status of species, that is, the state of their populations and the conservation measures to adopt.
Melanism: Genetic phenomenon producing totally black animals.
Middle ear: Portion of the ear where the osselets (in mammals) are found, situated behind the tympanum.
Pheromone: Substance emitted by an animal which plays a role in the communication between individuals.
Phylogeny: Evolutionary family of a group of living things.
Polymorphism: Presence of different forms (called morphs) within the same species.
Range: The geographic area within which a species is present.
Rhinarium: Hairless area situated at the tip of the snout where the nostrils open; corresponds to the dog's nose.
Secondary sexual characteristic: Characteristic unique to each sex excluding genital organs. For example, the lion's mane is a secondary sexual characteristic.
Sexual dimorphism: Presence within a species of a male form and a female form of different physical characteristics.
Sexual maturity: Stage at which an animal is capable of reproducing.
Territory: Area in which an animal lives, hunts, and reproduces. It indicates to the other members of the species the limits of its territory by visual and olfactory markings and emissions of sound.
Tympanic bubble: Structure of the skull containing the internal and middle portions of the ear.
Vomeronasal organ: A sensory organ situated at the ceiling of the bucal cavity allowing the detection of certain molecules. It complements the olfactory organ.

Bibliography

Books

General works

M. Bouchner, *Guide des traces d'animaux*, Hatier, 1988
P.-P. Grassé, *Précis de zoologie : Vertébrés*. 3. Reproduction, biologie, évolution et systématique. Oiseaux et mammifères. Masson, 1977

Works on felines and carnivores

R. Dallet, *Les Félins*, Nathan, 1992
R.F. Ewer, *The Carnivores*, Cornell University Press, 1973

J.L. Gittleman (sous la direction de), *Carnivore Behavior, Ecology and Evolution*, Cornell University Press, 1989
J. Scott, *Le Royaume des lions*, Nathan, 1995
J. Seidensticker et S. Lumpkin (sous la direction de), *Les Félins*, Bordas, 1992

Guides to fauna

B. Bousquet, *Guide des parcs nationaux d'Afrique. Afrique du Nord, Afrique de l'ouest*, Delachaux et Niestlé, 1992
T. Haltenorth et H. Diller, *Mammifères d'Afrique et de Madagascar*, Delachaux et Niestlé, 1985
D. Macdonald et P. Barrett, *Guide complet de mammifères de France et d'Europe*, Delachaux et Niestlé, 1995
F. Thille, M. Breuil et J.-P. Mayeur, *Animaux du Kenya et de la Tanzanie*, l'Harmattan, 1993

Travel guides

J.N. Darde, et J. Kahane, *Guide des saisons et des climats à l'usage de tous les voyageurs*, Balland, 1989
G. Crowther et *al.*, *Africa*, Lonely Planet, 1995 (in English)
Le Grand Guide des safaris africains, collection Bibliothèque du voyageur, Gallimard, 1991

Guides classified by country

BELIZE:
A. Bradbury, *Guide to Belize*, Bradt, (in English)
Mexique-Guatemala, collection Guide du routard, Hachette

BRAZIL:
D. Camus et C. Manoncourt, *Brésil*, Collection Grands voyages, guides Arthaud
A. Draffen et *al.*, *Brésil*, Lonely Planet
Brésil, collection Guide du routard, Hachette

INDIA:
G. Crowther et *al.*, *Inde*, Lonely Planet
Inde, Ladakh, Bhoutan, Guide bleu, Hachette

INDONESIA:
D. Basdevant, *En Indonésie*, Guides Visa, Hachette
Le Grand Guide de l'Indonésie, collection Bibliothèque du voyageur, Gallimard
Indonésie, collection Guide du routard, Hachette
E. Richard et A. Vicart, *Indonésie*, Guide Arthaud

KENYA:
G. Crowther et H. Finlay, *Kenya*, Guide Arthaud
Kenya, Nelles Guides

NAMIBIA.
Le Grand Guide de la Namibie, collection Bibliothèque du voyageur, Gallimard

NEPAL:
Inde du Nord-Népal-Tibet, collection Guide du routard, Hachette
T. Wheeler et R. Everist, *Népal*, Lonely Planet

SENEGAL:
A. Arvel, *Sénégal*, Guide Arthaud
Au Sénégal, Guide Visa, Hachette
Le Grand Guide du Sénégal, collection Bibliothèque du voyageur, Gallimard
J.C. Klotchkooff, *Sénégal*, Guide Marcus

UNITED STATES:
Le Grand Guide des Rocheuses, collection Bibliothèque du voyageur, Gallimard

ZIMBABWE:
Afrique australe, Guide de poche-Voyage, Marcus
D. Swaney, *Zimbabwe, Botswana and Namibia*, Lonely Planet (in English)

Videocassettes

Léopard en famille, BBC/Canal+, 1987

Chasseurs de ténèbres, BBC, 1995

Les Lions d'Etosha, National Geographic Video

La vie sauvage africaine (parc d'Etosha), National Geographic Video, 1980

The Velvet Claw: A Natural History of the Carnivores, BBC, 1993

CD-Roms

Big Cats, Ransom, 1996
Anglo-Saxon references are available from Natural History Books Services.

Index of species

Geographic index

Sources of illustrations

Y. ARTHUS-BERTRAND (STOCK IMAGE) : p. 40-41
A. BEIGNET : p. 64, 65 b, 66
S. BONNEAU : p. 99, 104, 105
J.-M. CRESTO (STOCK IMAGE) : p. 45, 78 h
DANI/JESKE (BIOS) : p. 61 h, 87 h
J.-P. FERRERO (PHO.N.E.) : p. 6, 14, 87 b
J.-P. FERRERO/J.-M. LABAT (PHO.N.E.) : couverture, p. 16, 17, 18-19, 22-23, 47 h, 47 b, 52 h, 58, 71, 118
T. FIELD (STOCK IMAGE) : p. 48
F. GOHIER (PHO.N.E.) : p. 10, 91 h, 94-95, 106-107
M. GRENET/ A. SOUMILLARD (PHO.N.E.) : p. 15, 54-55
O. GRUNEWALD : p. 68-69, 73, 100, 113, 114 h, 114 b, 121
M. GUNTHER (BIOS) : p. 78 b
M. HARVEY/FOTONATURE (BIOS) : p. 85
J.-F. HELLIO/N. VAN INGEN (PHO.N.E.) : p. 92
C. JARDEL (PHO.N.E.) : p. 116-117
P. JULLIEN (STOCK IMAGE) : p. 115
J.-M. LABAT (PHO.N.E.) : p. 61 b, 62 h, 62 b, 89
F. LECUYER : p. 20, 75, 76
C. et R. MARION : p. 8-9, 21, 51 h, 51 b, 53, 64 h, 93
H. REINHARD (PHO.N.E.) : p. 29, 35, 111
SEITRE (BIOS) : p. 88
STOCK IMAGE : 63, 80-81
R. VALTER (PHO.N.E.) : p. 101
A. VISAGE (PHO.N.E.) : p. 91 h
P. WEIMANN (BIOS) : p. 12